the manchester city Football Club
Official Pictorial History 1880-1997

Superbia in Proelio

Concilio et Labore

Managing Editor
Mike Hill

Assistant Editor
John Maddocks

Associate Editor
Joanne Parker (MCFC)

Design
Nick Cooper

Photographs supplied by:
Manchester Evening News Picture Library, Diverse Media Picture Library, John Maddocks Private Collection, Manchester City FC Picture Library, Manchester Central Reference Library Local Studies Unit, Colorsport & Hulton-Getty.
If the book has inadvertently breached any person's or organisation's copyright, our sincere apologies. Please contact Diverse Media if you wish to take the matter further.

Acknowledgements
Diverse Media would like to thank - amongst many others - Steve Anglesey (editor, City Magazine), Judy and Alan in the MEN Picture Library, Rita on the MEN Picture Desk, Joanne Parker, Geoff Durbin and Mick Peek at MCFC, Geoff Proffitt, Ted Stanfield and Andrew Webb in MEN Production.

Published by
Diverse Media Ltd, 164 Deansgate, Manchester M60 2RD.
tel: 0161-839 1416
fax: 0161-839 1488
e-mail: citylife@mcr1.poptel.org.uk

First published in November 1997. Printed and bound by Polar Print, Leicester (0116) 261 0800.

ISBN 0 9529086 1 1

Blue Velvet

Broadcaster James H. Reeve, a Manchester City supporter through thick and thin since 1955, who was at Newcastle for the championship decider in 1968, at Wembley in 1976 for the last Cup triumph, and the star of many a Junior Blues pantomime since, ponders on the peculiar significance of Manchester City, its supporters, its colours and its place in the overall scheme of things.

It was probably a result of the panic brought on by the approach of the deadline for the delivery of these few words, but with a handful of days remaining, I awoke in the small hours. The radio was still on, and, already bewildered, I was startled to hear the World Service continuity bloke say to people in many continents: "And I speak as a Manchester City supporter: always the optimist."

I had missed whatever prompted the remark, but the fact that it was uttered was simultaneously surprising and perfectly understandable. Why should a man working a night-shift, presumably with all the sense of isolation and futility that brings, feel the need to say such a thing, knowing that almost everyone who would understand it would be fast asleep?

Perhaps it was a way of reaching out to the listeners, to the war-torn, the famine-stricken, the oppressed and the snowbound, to tell them that the human spirit is indefatigable and that others, too, have known hardship. The trouble with that theory is that it's not a metaphor which is likely to be grasped immediately in, say, Mogadishu.

> There is something about us which does manifest itself in an equanimity towards Kipling's twin imposters, success and failure.

But I know why the man felt he had to say it. He believed it to be a statement about himself. It was a declaration of stoicism, tinged with perversity, of defiance laced with self-deprecation, an attitude which is deemed honourable in many cultures. Of course, that is a convenient pose to strike during the present brief period of restructuring and consolidation.

In the - temporarily absent - glory days, it was a matter for quiet pride and modest exultation, and one assumes that such a state of affairs will be restored very shortly, but even then there was something faintly quirky about being a Blue.

Let's not get carried away. There are affable and patient people amongst the supporters of all clubs, and it must be said that not every City fan is the embodiment of chivalry and Corinthianism at all times, so I don't think we can claim to be uniquely or exclusively noble about it all. Yet there is something about us which does manifest itself in an equanimity towards Kipling's twin imposters, success and failure, allowing for the occasional fit of exasperation.

One explanation may lie in the psychology of colours. Sky Blue is not an aggressive or vainglorious or men-

James H. Reeve drags himself up on stage for the Junior Blues Panto 1994.

acing shade. I can think of no significant historical armies which have opted for it. It doesn't make any promises.

So much the better then when City prove to be an iron fist in a pastel glove: so much more bearable when the effect is appropriately powder-puff. And whatever colour modern dyestuffs produce or sponsors demand, there is a sort of hazy blue karma about the proceedings which seems to span the generations.

Does this mean that a certain type of person becomes a City fan, or *vice versa*? I like to think it is a sort of gradual process of homogenisation.

Certainly, the impartial observer seems to find us agreeable and worthy of curious admiration. I suspect that is why one of the 20th century's greatest embezzlers (Nick Leeson) thought it entirely appropriate to sport his City shirt on his way to lengthy imprisonment. To wear the colours of a more presumptuous club might have been in bad taste: to declare oneself a Blue seemed to rather take the edge off it.

And, bearing in mind a little local difficulty which does make our position somewhat exceptional, I think we might compare ourselves to Canadians. This is our lot, resulting from a decision taken long ago, and we shall stand by it, conducting ourselves with rather more decorum than our brash neighbours, knowing that we are essentially in the right.

I hope that these pictures of strong men in the strange and splendid Sky Blue, whilst maybe not providing an explanation, will at least confirm the legitimacy of our noble conviction. Born out of the throes of bankruptcy 117 years ago, Manchester City march towards the 21st century confident that fans yet unborn will recognise that the club's fortunes mirror real life all too clearly.

A photograph is worth a thousand words they reckon, but most people just glance cursorily at pictures, failing to 'read' them as they would a chunk of words. Take the photo on this page: one of the reasons many previous books have incorrectly thought this was Maine Road being constructed is because they didn't 'read' it.

First, the mill and factory chimneys indicate an industrial setting, not a residential one. The Hyde Road ground was in an area of Manchester known as 'the workshop of the world', surrounded by 'dark Satanic mills': Moss Side and Fallowfield was - and still is - mainly residential. Secondly, the large building to the left is recognisably the Ellen Wilkinson High School. Thirdly, the dress of the construction workers is late-Victorian (bowler hats, not flat caps), and the earth removal method is by temporary rail tracks, without the use of the internal combustion engine.

Very often, the way to gain most from the photographs in this book is to look at the backgrounds, the peripheries, the fashions and styles of the people captured for posterity. For example, just look at the footwear of the players over the years, from ordinary plimsolls to basketball boots to expensive, state-of-the-art, fashionable, sponsored trainers.

To produce this book, we trawled through thousands of photos, many in poor condition, mis-filed or both. A lot have been stolen, or lost, or were thrown away at a time when 'heritage' was deemed old-fashioned and/or irrelevant (Manchester City's picture library is the poorer for Peter Swales ordering the archives to be thrown away). Some things soon became quite apparent: first, not many photos exist from the early years, but the biggest gap is the 1940s, when newsprint rationing meant local newspapers didn't take many photos. Second, colour photos were only very slowly adopted by national and local papers, so the black & white picture prospered until well into the '80s. Thirdly, overseas games and games played under floodlights usually produced poor photos.

But, nonetheless, we hope we have managed to find a range of quality photographs which cover the history of this great Mancunian institution, and which, when supported by the captions, will leave all readers with a greater understanding of and respect for the club we all love and support - through the good times and the bad times - with a passion beyond reason.

Finally, the many people who helped produce this book are thanked on page 4, but it does no harm to thank them all again.

1880 The club was formed as West Gorton St Mark's and this was the name of the club until...

1884 ...when it became Gorton AFC.

1887 The name was changed again to Ardwick FC and the club moved to Hyde Road.

1891 Ardwick played in the Football Alliance, which became Division Two of the Football League in...

1892 ...when Ardwick finished 5th in their first season.

1894 A bankrupt Ardwick ceased to exist, and from the ashes rose the phoenix called Manchester City FC.

1899 P34 W23 D6 L5: 92 goals for, 35 against, gave City promotion to Division One as champions. Leading scorer was Welsh international Billy Meredith with 29 goals, including four hat-tricks. Not bad for a winger!

1900 Manchester MP and Prime Minister, A.J.Balfour, visited Hyde Road on 29 September to watch City beat Stoke 2-0.

1902 The Blues were relegated along with Birmingham City.

1903 City bounced back first time as champions, scoring 95 goals in 34 games. Top scorer was Billy Gillespie with 30.

1904 At the Crystal Palace, City won the FA Cup for the first time, beating Bolton Wanderers 1-0. Scorer of the only goal was Meredith. The Blues also finished runners-up in the League, scoring more goals (71) than any other club.

1905 The football world was shaken when Billy Meredith was found guilty of offering a £10 bribe to Aston Villa's full-back Leake so that City would have a better chance of winning the game. The Welshman was suspended for a year.

1906 The club was heavily punished by the FA for paying players more than the permitted rate. Various officials were either banned for life or suspended, and the club was ordered to transfer 17 players after they had finished their own suspensions.

1909 Relegation once again as City went down with Leicester City.

1910 The Blues were Second Division champions for the third time and embarked on the club's first Continental tour: five games were played in Germany, Denmark and Sweden, four of which were won.

1915 In the Lancashire Section of the Wartime League, City won both the principal and subsidiary tournaments.

1919 Legendary sportsman Max Woosnam joined the Blues as an amateur.

1920 King George V attended the game between City and Liverpool on 27 March at Hyde Road.

1921 City were runners-up in Division One to champions Burnley.

1923 Following a disastrous fire at Hyde Road in November 1920, City moved to the present headquarters at Maine Road and won the first game 2-1 against Sheffield United. Horace Barnes and Tommy Johnson were the scorers.

1925 The highly-influential player Jimmy McMullan was signed by the Blues.

The now defunct City Gates pub, virtually a City museum when former City hero George Heslop was the landlord in the 1980s. When it was the Hyde Road Hotel, it was the pub in which Manchester City FC was born in 1894, and the Hyde Road ground was at the rear.

1926 City were FA Cup finalists having scored 31 goals in six games before losing 0-1 to Bolton Wanderers in the Final. To complete a disappointing season, they were also relegated.

1927 Amazingly City missed promotion by 1/200th of a goal, even though they won 8-0 on the last day of the season. They were pipped by Portsmouth. Three famous names were signed in this year: Eric Brook, Fred Tilson and Bobby Marshall. Between them they would go on to make over 1000 League appearances for City.

1928 Division Two champions for the fourth time. Top of the scoring charts was Frank Roberts who cracked in 20 of the 100 goals netted.

1929 Tommy Johnson established a club scoring record which still stands today. He scored 38 League goals, including five against Everton in one game. Future Manchester United manager (Sir) Matt Busby joined City as an inside-forward.

Tommy Johnson, City's record goal-scorer, happily recalls his playing days.

1933 City were FA Cup finalists once more, losing 0-3 to Everton.

1934 FA Cup winners, this time by beating Portsmouth 2-1. Fred Tilson scored twice to add to the seven he registered on the way to Wembley. Overcome with emotion, young goalkeeper Frank Swift fainted at the end of the game.

1935 The brilliant Peter Doherty signed for City from Blackpool. In later years, older supporters would discuss for hours who was the better player: Peter, or Colin Bell.

1937 City won the First Division championship for the first time, undefeated for the last 22 matches of the season. Northern Ireland international Peter Doherty scored 30 goals.

1938 Unbelievably City were relegated, despite scoring 80 goals, more than any other club in the First Division! Eric Westwood joined City, the start of a 14-year association.

1946 Former City favourite Sam Cowan was appointed manager. Manchester United share Maine Road until 1948-9.

1947 The Blues gained promotion to the First Division following the Second World War. Thanks to an appalling winter, the final League game was at Maine Road on 14 June. Roy Clarke made his City debut and George Smith scored all five of City's goals.

1949 The club signed former German prisoner-or-war Bert Trautmann who would go of to make 545 League and cup appearances for the Blues.

1950 Innovative manager and former Blue Les McDowall was appointed and signed that great Welsh wing-half, Roy Paul, after the club had been relegated. Skilful players both, Ivor Broadis and Don Revie joined City.

1953 Floodlights were installed at Maine Road and a series of evening friendly games played. The first visitors were Hearts, from Edinburgh.

1955 City reached the FA Cup Final for the first time in 21 years, losing 1-3 to Newcastle United and playing most of the game with 10 men following a serious injury to the late Jimmy Meadows. On the way to Wembley they beat Manchester United, and also did a League double over the Reds, winning 5-0 at Old Trafford. The mercurial Scottish inside-forward Bobby Johnstone arrived from Hibernian.

City captain Roy Paul triumphantly holds aloft the FA Cup in 1956 which he had sworn he would do when the Blues were beaten the previous year.

1956 Successful this time round, City won the FA Cup by beating Birmingham City 3-1 and despite goalkeeper Bert Trautmann playing the latter stages of the second half with a broken neck!

1957 A new plan introduced by Les McDowall all went pear-shaped. Twin centre-halves were supposed to stiffen the defence. The team lost 1-6 at Preston North End, then 2-9 at West Bromwich Albion. The plan was shelved. Ken Barnes scored a hat-trick of penalties against Everton at Maine Road and another penalty in the return fixture at Goodison.

1958 A unique sight in the Goals column at the end of the season: City scored 104 and let in 100!

1959 City avoided relegation in the very last match of the season.

1960 The Blues created a new British transfer record by spending £55,000 on Denis Law from Huddersfield Town.

1961 Denis Law scored all six of City's goals in a 6-1 FA Cup 'victory' at Luton. The referee abandoned the game and City lost the replay, 1-3. Law scored again.

1962 Glyn Pardoe became City's youngest-ever League debutant in April when he played against Birmingham City. He was 15 years and 314 days old.

1963 City were relegated to Division Two thanks to a Manchester United victory in the derby and, due to fixture congestion following a terrible winter, completed three FA Cup rounds in 11 days. Les McDowall was sacked and George Poyser appointed manager.

The heartbreaker! Former United star Denis Law scores the only goal of the 1974 Old Trafford derby game... for City. He never kicked a ball in anger again.

1964 Northern Ireland international Johnny Crossan was signed. He was to be a valuable asset in the 1965-66 season.

1965 City's lowest-ever League attendance, 8,015 against Swindon Town. Swindon won and one of their scorers was a young Michael Summerbee. The club employed Joe Mercer as manager and he asked a brilliant coach, Malcolm Allison, to work alongside him. Their first signings were Ralph Brand and... Mike Summerbee. An up-and-coming lad made his City bow at Cardiff on a Friday night. Mike Doyle went on to appear 558 times in City's colours in senior games.

1966 The Blues won promotion as champions for the sixth time with 14 goals from Neil Young and 13 from Summerbee, and City captured Bury's Colin Bell. His career was a sparkling one, and he holds the club record for England caps awarded, 48. In the summer, Allison insisted the club buy Tony Book. Tony skippered City through the forthcoming glory years and remained connected with the club in various capacities until 1996.

1967 The last piece of the Mercer/Allison jig-saw was slotted in when Francis Lee arrived from Bolton for around £60,000.

1968 City's second First Division Championship with 58 points from 42 games! The club's regular XI were all English. The Charity Shield joined the other silverware as West Bromwich Albion were demolished 6-1 at Maine Road. A big disappointment in the European Cup, however, as City learned about European football the hard way. They went out at the first hurdle against Turkish champions, Fenerbahce.

1969 FA Cup winners again after beating Leicester City 1-0 thanks to a brilliant Neil Young goal. Youngster Willie Donachie arrived from Glasgow to carve out a great career at City.

1970 A superb double was achieved: City won the League Cup by beating West Bromwich Albion at Wembley 2-1 in extra time, then later the same season they won the European Cup-Winners Cup, beating Poland's Gornik Zabrze by the same score in Vienna.

1971 Allison was appointed manager with Joe Mercer taking the post of General Manager. The club reached the semi-finals of the Cup Winners' Cup, eliminated finally by Chelsea over two legs.

1972 City won the Charity Shield for the third time, beating Aston Villa 1-0. The Blues spent £200,000 in acquiring Rodney Marsh from QPR but it was a controversial buy. However gifted the player was, there were those who reckoned that the timing of his arrival cost City the championship.

1973 Allison left the Blues and former player Johnny Hart took over as manager. Ill-health forced him to retire and new chairman Peter Swales and the Board invited Ron Saunders to take up the reins. Denis Law returned to City for one season, and sent United down with a back-heeled goal.

1974 The Blues were League Cup Finalists, losing 1-2 to Wolves. Saunders was dismissed and former City full-back and skipper Tony Book took over. Asa Hartford joined City for the first of two spells with the Blues.

1976 Revenge for the 1955 Cup Final defeat by beating Newcastle United 2-1 in the League Cup Final, becoming one of only three sides to have won the trophy twice. Peter Barnes and Dennis Tueart were the scorers. One of the club's stalwarts left to take over at Chester City as player-manager, 'Mr Dependable' Alan Oakes. A model professional, Alan turned out over 1000 times for City at various levels.

1977 City finished runners-up to Liverpool in the First Division, the club having bought Mike Channon for this campaign.

1978 The Reserves won the Central League for the first time, and the club installed undersoil heating.

1979 Malcolm Allison returned to City and the club paid out a record fee - nearly £1.5m - for Wolves' Steve Daley. The youth team reached the final of the FA Youth Cup and lost 0-2 on aggregate to Millwall.

1980 The youth team again reached the final of the same competition only to lose 2-3 on aggregate to Aston Villa. In October, John Bond moved into the manager's chair and arrested an alarming slide in the club's fortunes. He raised the team to a safe spot in the table in 1981...

1981 ... and also made City Centenary FA Cup Finalists, losing 2-3 to Spurs in a replay. Tommy Hutchison scored at both ends in the first game! Paul Power scored a magnificent winner in the Villa Park semi-final over Ipswich Town. The Blues also reached the semi-final of the League Cup. Kevin Reeves cost the club over £1m. Million pound-plus signing Trevor Francis scored twice on his debut at Stoke City.

1983 Relegation to Division Two in the last minute of the season! Luton Town's Raddy Antic hit the deciding goal and manager David Pleat celebrated all over the Maine Road pitch as City went down and Luton were saved. Manager Bond had resigned earlier in the season and John Benson was sacked at the end.

1985 City were promoted to the First Division under Billy McNeill and Jimmy Frizzell, having finished in third place. The Youth team won the Lancashire Youth Cup for the fourth consecutive year.

City's most expensive player at the time and first million pound signing, Steve Daley, seen here in a tussle for the ball with future Blue, Southampton's Graham Baker.

1986 Billy McNeill left for Aston Villa and Jimmy Frizzell took over. The Blues reached the first Full Members Cup Final, losing 4-5 to Chelsea. The club won the FA Youth Cup beating Manchester United over two legs on aggregate, and watched by a total of 25,700 fans. The A team won the First Division of the Lancashire League, losing only one game in 36 and scoring 132 goals.

1987 Mel Machin took over as manager but again City were relegated to Division Two. There was a highlight in the season, however, the 10-1 thrashing of Huddersfield Town at Maine Road. There were hat-tricks for Paul Stewart, Tony Adcock and David White. The Reserves won the Central League for the second time.

1988 Paul Stewart was sold to Tottenham Hotspur for a fee of £1.7m.

1989 Promotion was achieved under Mel Machin. The youth team reached the final of the FA Youth Cup but lost 1-2 to Watford after extra time in the second leg. Clive Allen was signed in the 1989 close season for £1m from Bordeaux. Major highlight of the 1989-90 season was when in September the Blues trounced Manchester United at Maine Road, 5-1. City appoint their fifth manager in seven years as Howard Kendall takes charge. He was to stay just 11 months before walking out to join Everton.

1990 City spent £1m in purchasing goalkeeper Tony Coton from Watford, and another popular arrival was Niall Quinn from Arsenal. The Youth team won the Lancashire Cup for the 9th time....

1991 ....and then for the tenth! Peter Reid was now club manager. Defender Keith Curle moved to Maine Road from Wimbledon for a record fee of £2.5m, and veteran midfield player Steve McMahon joined City from Liverpool. David White scored four at Villa Park, the first time a City player had achieved this target since Brian Kidd in the 1970s against Leicester City. The club's A and B teams both finish runners-up in their respective divisions of the Lancashire League.

1992 Again City went to Wimbledon and spent £2.5m on a defender, this time full-back Terry Phelan. The new Umbro stand was opened at the Platt Lane end of the ground.

1993 Brian Horton was installed as manager.

1994 After a long campaign, former player Francis Lee took over from Peter Swales as chairman, and work began to build an all-seater Kippax Stand. Brian Horton signed three players who not only ensured City's place in the top flight but were also tremendous crowd-pleasers. They were Uwe Rosler from Germany, Paul Walsh from Portsmouth, and Peter Beagrie from Everton. Nicky Summerbee, son of Mike, also joined the Blues.

1995 Alan Ball was appointed manager. Chairman Francis Lee showed his determination in bringing quality players to Maine Road by paying Dynamo Tbilisi £2m for the vastly-talented Gio Kinkladze. Another newcomer was Kit Symons from Portsmouth. Youth coach Neil McNab saw his youth side win the Lancashire League Division Two. Bert Trautmann formally opened the new Kippax stand.

1996 City were relegated in May and Alan Ball resigned early the following season. Steve Coppell took over as manager with Phil Neal as his assistant, but after only a few weeks Coppell resigned on health grounds. Phil Neal became caretaker-manager. Frank Clark was appointed manager on 29 December. New players were brought in and a safe position in the First Division was secured. The immensely gifted Paul Lake was forced to retire after a long battle against serious injury.

1997 The club ended its long association with Umbro and signed a deal with Italian sports kit manufacturers Kappa.

Wilf Wild	1932-46	
Sam Cowan	17.11.46 - 24.06.47	*Resigned*
Jock Thomson	12.11.47 - 29.04.50	*Resigned*
Les McDowall	1.06.50 - 28.05.63	*Resigned*
George Poyser	11.06.63 - 16.04.65	*Resigned*
Joe Mercer	13.07.65 - 10.71	*To General Manager*
Malcolm Allison	0.71 - 30.03.73	*Resigned*
John Hart	30.03.73 - 11.73	*Resigned*
Ron Saunders	11.1973 - 11.04.74	*Dismissed*
Tony Book	11.04.74 - 9.10.80	*Dismissed*
John Bond	13.10.80 - 3.02.83	*Resigned*
John Benson	3.02.83 - 05.83	*Dismissed*
Billy McNeill	0.06.83 - 22.09.86	*Resigned*
Jimmy Frizzell	1.10.86 - 22.05.87	*To General Manager*
Mel Machin	22.05.87 - 26.11.89	*Dismissed*
Howard Kendall	11.12.89 - 6.11.90	*Resigned*
Peter Reid	15.11.90 - 09.93	*Dismissed*
Brian Horton	10.93 - 15.05.95	*Dismissed*
Alan Ball	3.07.95 - 26.08.96	*Resigned*
Steve Coppell	7.10.96 - 8.11.96	*Resigned*
Phil Neal	8.11.96 - 29.12.96	*Resigned*
Frank Clark	30.12.96	

Division One Championship: 1937, 1968

Division One Runners-Up: 1904, 1921, 1977

Division Two Championship: 1899, 1903, 1910, 1928, 1947, 1966

Division Two Runners-Up: 1896, 1951, 1989

Division Two Third Place: 1985

European Cup-Winners Cup, Winners: 1970

FA Cup Winners: 1904, 1934, 1956, 1969

FA Cup Finalists: 1926, 1933, 1955, 1981

Football League Cup Winners: 1970, 1976

Football League Cup Finalists: 1974

Full Members Cup Finalists: 1986

FA Charity Shield Winners: 1937, 1968, 1972

FA Charity Shield Finalists: 1934, 1956, 1969, 1973

Lancashire Senior Cup Winners: 1921, 1923, 1928, 1930, 1953, 1974

Lancashire Senior Cup Finalists: 1897, 1924, 1932

Manchester Senior Cup Winners: 1892, 1901, 1903, 1907, 1911, 1928, 1929, 1932, 1933, 1949

Manchester Senior Cup Finalists: 1898, 1902, 1924, 1925, 1926, 1930, 1934, 1950, 1958, 1962, 1964

FA Youth Cup Winners: 1986

FA Youth Cup Finalists: 1979, 1980, 1989

Lancashire Youth Cup Winners: 1973, 1977, 1980, 1982, 1983, 1984, 1985, 1989, 1990, 1992

Lancashire Youth Cup Finalists: 1981, 1995

Lancashire Combination, Division One Champions: 1902

'Top of the Class!' Three graduates from the 1986 Youth Cup winning side, Ian Brightwell, Andy Hinchcliffe and Paul Lake celebrate Andy's rocket header in the 5-1 drubbing of Manchester United in 1989. And Lakey, your Blue bias is showing.

We're on our way' thinks Mike Summerbee as he hits home City's first in the championship-winning game at Newcastle in 1968.

Lancashire Combination, Division One Runners-Up: 1899, 1903

Lancashire Combination, Division Two Champions: 1909

Central League Champions: 1978, 1987

Central League Runners-Up: 1922, 1931

Central League, Division Two Fourth Place *(Promoted):* 1984

Healey Charity Cup Winners: 1898, 1899, 1901

Manchester League Runners-Up: 1952, 1955

Gilgryst Cup Winners: 1939, 1951

Lancashire League Division One Winners: 1986

Lancashire League Division Two Principle Competition Winners: 1967, 1969, 1995

Lancashire League Division Two Supplementary Competition Winners: 1958, 1967, 1968 *(shared with Liverpool)*

Lancashire League Division Two Supplementary Competition Runners-Up: 1956, 1970

Hereford Senior Cup *(by invitation):* 1980

World War One

Lancashire Section Principle Tournament Winners: 1915

Lancashire Section Subsidiary Tournament Winners: 1915, 1919

Manchester City (0) v Bolton Wanderers (1) at Wembley in 1926. A near miss! The Bolton goal-keeper - obviously weighed down by that jersey and his boots - has been unable to cut out the cross from the City left-winger, and the next attack will be launched from the opposite flank. Anybody know the identity of the City player trying to rip down the net in his frustration?

Unsuccessful at Wembley the previous season, City returned in 1934. Shaken by an early Portsmouth goal, they rallied to the Blue cause and here Freddy Tilson, partially hidden by a Pompey defender, manages to squeeze the ball into the net. Later he fired home the winner to bring the FA Cup to Maine Road.

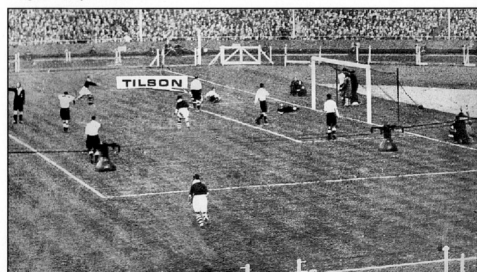

Newcastle United's Ronnie Simpson in the 1954 Cup Final couldn't prevent this rocket from Scottish international Bobby Johnstone from rattling the back of the net. The Magpies won the Final 3-1. Incidentally, when the Scottish international scored at Wembley the following season against Birmingham City, he became the first man to score in consecutive FA Cup finals.

The clincher! Inside-left Jack Dyson wheels away in triumph to be congratulated by Don Revie after scoring City's third goal in the 1956 Cup Final. Winger Roy Clarke also celebrates as the Blues beat Birmingham City 3-1. Dyson was also a county cricketer for Lancashire and the end of the football season coincided with the start of the cricket season.

A youthful Franny Lee somehow finds the energy to haul a boot out of the Wembley gluepot (caused by the Horse of the Year show) and smacks a pass into the West Brom penalty area. The Blues were already weary from travelling back from a Cup-Winners' Cup tie in Portugal played three days earlier and must have shuddered when they saw this pitch.

In the 1969 Cup Final, Leicester City defenders Rodrigues and Woollett look on anxiously as Neil Young's blistering drive eludes young goalkeeper Peter Shilton. The centre had been supplied by Mike Summerbee after he left David Nish stranded near the touch-line and cut the ball back to Young. This only goal of the game opened the gateway into Europe for the Blues the following season.

A rarity - a Cup Final the Blues didn't win! Wolves were the victors in the1974 League Cup final but here Colin Bell put City back on even terms after Kenny Hibbitt had put Wolves in front. Denis Law - in his last season in professional football - and Rodney Marsh urge the ball into the net..

This was a night in 1970 when the weather ensured there were no favourites! Everybody was soaked in the incessant downpour, the players, officials, the UEFA dignitaries, the media and the fans! Vienna's Prater Stadium enjoyed no cover whatsoever from the elements, but that didn't stop the Blue Army going wild as Franny Lee's penalty beat Gornik Zabrze's keeper Kostka. City won the Cup-winner's Cup Final 2-1.

Joe Royle scored in every round in the 1976 League Cup competition and even had a 'goal' disallowed in this Final against Newcastle United. Peter Barnes scored in the first half and then this brilliant goal from Dennis Tueart sealed the game after the break, wiping out Alan Gowling's equaliser. Full marks too to defender Willie Donachie for his accurate free-kick.

And here is Barnes's goal in the first half. A cluster of Newcastle defenders were powerless to prevent the 1976 Young Footballer of the Year slamming the ball past keeper Mike Mahoney.

Gerry Gow plucks the ball out of the Tottenham net as Nicky Reid (no.4) leads the fans in celebrating a City goal in the 1981 FA Cup final replay. Steve MacKenzie rushes forward to add his congratulations to smothered scorer Kevin Reeves...

...But Spurs' Ricardo Villa overcame his disappointment at being substituted in the first game by cracking home the Tottenham equaliser past Joe Corrigan and the late Tommy Caton. It was hard luck on Joe as he'd made an excellent block save from Steve Archibald (far right). Another goal from the Argentinian gave Spurs a 3-2 victory.

The pipe-opener to the 1968-69
season and West Brom have just
been humiliated 6-1 by a rampant
Manchester City. George Heslop
proudly holds up the FA Charity
Shield and is followed up the
steps to the Directors' Box by
goalkeeper Ken Mulhearn, Glyn
Pardoe, Mike Doyle and Alan
Oakes. New signing Bobby Owen
made his City bow in this game
and celebrated by scoring two
excellent goals.

The doubting Thomases wrote off
the Full Members' Cup as a
Mickey Mouse competition and
predicted that the inaugural
Wembley final would be a flop.
How wrong they were! Over
65,000 fans turned up to see City
who had had to play Manchester
United 24 hours earlier - lose to
Chelsea by a narrow 4-5 score-
line. Here City's Mark Lillis holds
off Chelsea player.

Manchester City must have spent a small fortune on silver polish in 1968-69, but who cared?
Pictured here as though daring anyone to take these trophies off him is skipper Tony Book. On the
left is the beautifully ornate League Championship trophy, the FA Cup is in the centre, and the FA
Charity Shield completes the haul.

Apart from promotion from the Second Division, winning the FA Cup in 1904 was Manchester City's first major success. They were also First Division runners-up in the same season. The team was made up of Hillman, Burgess, McMahon, Frost, Hynds, Ashworth, Meredith, Livingstone, Gillespie, Turnbull and Booth.

Another shot from the same season, this time including the full professional squad. The shield below the FA Cup represented the Manchester Senior Cup of which City were joint holders.

There was no doubt that Sam Cowan's disappointment cut deeply at the end of the 1933 Cup Final, which City lost 0-3 to Everton. Life's ups and downs were vividly portrayed the following year, as we can see here. Sam gratefully received the trophy from King George V. Eric Brook waits to collect his medal.

"We'll be back next year," City skipper Sam Cowan allegedly promised King George V at the end of the 1933 Cup Final when the Blues lost 0-3 to Everton. And back they were, as you can see from this picture of Sam as he happily rides aloft a Finglands coach - the company still used by City 63 years later! - to display the FA Cup to happy fans.

City's first ever League Championship in 1937. They were undefeated from Christmas Day for 22 games to the end of the season. P42, W22, D13, L7. Goals for 107, against 61: City scored six in a game twice, and five in a game four times. They were relegated next season.

Joe Mercer raises the Cup that cheers to the cheers of the Maine Road faithful in 1968, surrounded by the players who brought the League Championship to Moss Side for the first time since 1937.

Hail the conquering heroes. The 1956 FA Cup winners show off the cup to the adoring fans from the back of a trusty Finglands coach.

Were you one of these four youngsters who proudly showed off the FA Charity Shield in 1968? They had just seen the Blues thrash West Brom 6-1, with newcomer Bobby Owen netting twice. Colin Bell looks slightly worried as the Shield moves away from his grasp!

No, Malcolm Allison hasn't taken up black magic and an interest in voodoo dolls. The Blues went to Sweden in the close season of 1972 and came out winners of a tournament for which this happy little fellow was the award. Meanwhile, Allison and Colin Bell are seeing if there's room for another City nameplate on the Charity Shield after the Blues had won it again pre-season.

A heaving crowd in Albert Square roars its delight as coach Dave Ewing (left) and Colin Bell show off the FA Cup in a triumphant homecoming in 1969. Behind Bell are Glyn Pardoe and Alan Oakes while captain Tony Book looks quite overcome by the whole affair. And how the facade of the buildings opposite the Town Hall has changed in 28 years!

Pitch invasions may be banned these days whatever the cause, but there was no stopping these triumphant Blues from sweeping on to the St James's Park turf the day City won the League in 1968. It's estimated that over 20,000 fans made the journey from Manchester to Tyneside to see the Blues win a hugely exciting game 4-3.

The stamina-sapping Wembley mud didn't stop Tony Book and his happy team-mates climbing the steps to the Royal Box to collect the League Cup and their tankards after the 1970 final. Slowly sinking into the morass under the weight of their skipper are Franny Lee and George Heslop, while Joe Corrigan appears to have burst into song to the dismay of Glyn Pardoe (right).

"Hope somebody's remembered to pick up my duty-free," thinks Tony Book, once more staggering under a large piece of silverware (European Cup-winners Cup) destined for the Maine Road boardroom. The rest of the happy fliers seem to have been well-organised.

City captain Mike Doyle removes the ribbon adorning the League Cup in Albert Square in 1976 to toss to the fans after he had lived up to the City banner at Wembley which proclaimed 'Doyle eats Magpies'! And hasn't PC 1603's sergeant told him to get his hair cut?

England and City defender Dave Watson was certainly in the wars in the 1976 League Cup final. And no, a Newcastle player hasn't pinched a winner's tankard (edge of picture). That's Dennis Tueart, who's swapped shirts with one of the opposition, Newcastle being his home team. City sub Kenny Clements joins in the triumphant procession round Wembley.

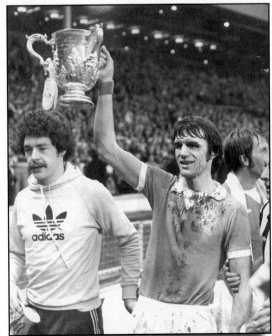

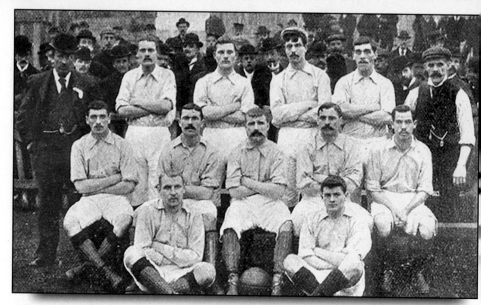

A City team prior to a match in the 1896-97 season. Bannister, Mann and McBride appear to have made the team despite their refusal to sport a distinguished moustache.

A City squad from around 1900 pose in front of the Grand Hotel. Third from right is 'Sandy' Turnbull, one of the players suspended in 1906 for accepting wages in excess of those permitted. He was transferred to Manchester United, and later was killed in the First World War.

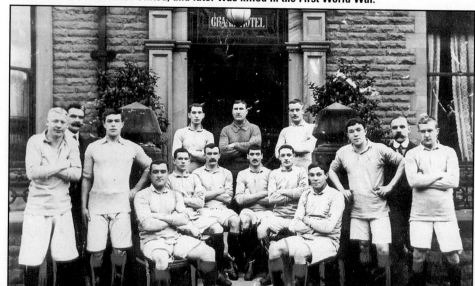

A ticket for the City v Newcastle United League game in October 1912. Before testimonial matches were introduced, players received the gate money (less expenses) for their benefit game. Bill Eadie came to City from Greenock Morton (1906-1914) and made, 204 league appearances, scoring six goals. Tom Kelso was signed from Third Lanark (1906-13), made 151 league appearances (he broke a collarbone in 1911/12), scoring three goals and winning one Scottish cap.

Moustaches were mainly out of favour when this squad photo was taken in the 1900s. It's a pity no record was kept which would enable us to identify the players 90 years later.

The players that the City board assembled after 1906 to replace all the ones suspended by the FA in that year, 17 in all. Irvine Thornley (seated left) would himself be suspended for irregularities concerning his transfer fee. The Hyde Road crowd illustrate that you couldn't get in unless you wore a cap!

Manchester City 1908-09. On the left (back row) are Harry Newbould, the Secretary-Manager, and club chairman W.A.Wilkinson. At the end of the line is trainer Bob Chatt.

The Blues in the last peacetime season before the 1914-18 war. Present are some players who would become stars of the 1920s, such as Tommy Browell and Horace Barnes. Striker Fred Howard can be seen on the second row of standing players, fifth from left. Fred scored four goals on his City debut against Liverpool.

The war was over and this is a team that turned out in 1919-20. Tommy Broad (front row) was the son of trainer Jimmy (back row). The legendary all-round sportsman Max Woosnam, who always carried a handkerchief tucked into a sleeve, was skipper. (*fourth from the right, back row*).

A gloomy Moss Side day when this was taken in the mid-1920s. In the background the old Scoreboard End (now the North Stand) can be seen, and in the top corner is a church where the City Megastore now stands.

The late Sir Matt Busby was a City player when this picture was taken in 1931. Originally an inside-forward, he eventually made his mark at right-half, and missed out on City's championship win in 1937 as he had been transferred to Liverpool.

Wearing their special Wembley strip, City proudly display the FA Cup, gained after beating Portsmouth 2-1. Freddy Tilson (seated, extreme left) scored both the City goals.

The City first team squad at the start of the 1935-36 campaign. It's to be hoped that the groundsman got around to cutting the grass before the season began!

No wonder the Blues are smiling! It's May 1937 and they've just won the First Division championship for the first time in the club's history. On the front row is Northern Ireland international Peter Doherty whose skills did so much to capture the trophy. By the way, where is it?

This is the side that gained promotion from the Second Division in 1947.
It was an unusual season in so far as it was necessary to extend it because of the appalling winter weather. Between City's penultimate and final League games they played two games in Ireland, and the last League game was on June 14th . Roy Clarke made his City debut and George Smith scored five goals.

In 1948-49, the Blues had two future successful managers in their team. Third from the right is Joe Fagan, who would guide Liverpool to a host of honours in later years, while in the middle of the front row is City skipper Les McDowall, who twice took the club to Wembley in the 1950s.

Enjoying the sunshine at Butlin's Holiday Camp in Filey, North Yorkshire in 1950 are a group of City players, joined on this photograph by Newcastle United's George Robledo (extreme right).

April 1956 and City display their FA Cup Final strip for the cameras. Clearly their expressions say that it's a winner, which is exactly what the Blues were against Birmingham City at Wembley. Now you know why the present North Stand used to be called the Scoreboard End.

City report back for training at the start of the 1958-59 season. How many of the older generation of fans can identify players like Roy Little, Ray Sambrook, Dave Ewing, and younger faces like Roy Cheetham and Alan Oakes?

The Blues report for training at the start of the 1956-57 campaign, manager Les McDowell still pleased with the Wembley visit the previous season which brought the FA Cup north. One famous face is missing… Bert Trautmann, the legendary City keeper who broke his neck in the Cup Final. Roy Paul (14) appears to be telling colleague Ken Barnes what he did on his holidays. Check out the plimsolls!

"Now this is a ball," manager George Poyser seems to be telling his players in the early '60s. Goalkeeper Harry Dowd (fourth from right) doesn't believe him, while the rest of the players including Mike Doyle, Dave Connor and Phil Burrows, think that the boss is joking.

All those years of trampolining practice in the Maine Road gym clearly paid off as the delirious trio of coach Dave Ewing, physio Peter Blakey and manager Joe Mercer celebrate a City goal in the 1970 League Cup final. The gentlemen on the adjoining bench however seem less than enthusiastic and distinctly short on happiness.

On the same wavelength: the perfect management team of Joe Mercer and Malcolm Allison discuss a tactical change in the League game against Newcastle United in October 1970.

The City fans packed around the tunnel end at Wembley greet their favourites as manager Ron Saunders (looking like an extra from *The Sweeney*) leads them out at the start of the 1974 League Cup final. Gripping the City presentation pennant firmly is Mike Summerbee, while Willie Donachie and Mike Doyle take a good look at the famous Wembley turf. Goalkeeper Keith Macrae appears to be more concerned with asking for divine help from above. He didn't get it.

Manager Johnny Hart who succeeded Malcolm Allison in the spring of 1973, firstly as caretaker-manager and then as manager. Johnny first played for the Blues during World War Two and, despite many injuries, played for the club throughout his career, even turning out as the A team goalkeeper in the 1960s! Sadly ill-health forced his retirement as manager.

The AC Milan fans were so upset after City drew with them in the San Siro stadium in November 1978 that the riot police, complete with rubber bullets and tear gas, were called out to protect the Blues. Looking for the quickest way to the airport after this UEFA Cup tie are coach Bill Taylor, manager Tony Book and physio Roy Bailey, together with the team's duty free.

"We're gonna terrify them in Europe!" Coach Malcolm Allison addresses the troops at the start of training in 1968, semi-naked and from the centre of the pitch (cf Les McDowell, page 45). Sadly the words were to haunt Big Mal as the Blues tumbled out at the first hurdle against Turkish champions Fenerbahce.

Win, lose or draw, City's fans are winners when it comes to greeting the team after a big occasion, and the occasion didn't come any bigger in 1981 than the FA Cup final. Led by the cigar-chewing John Bond, here Paul Power, Dennis Tueart, Nicky Reid, Steve MacKenzie, Bobby McDonald and Kevin Reeves acknowledge the fans' applause outside Maine Road after the Blues had lost the replay against Spurs.

John Bond had gone, along with former City player and short-time boss John Benson, so the reins were taken up by Billy McNeill who had captained Celtic to European Cup victory back in 1967. One of his first signings was mid-fielder Neil McNab who had once been Tottenham's youngest player and was with Brighton when the Blues signed him. His sons, twins Neil jnr. and Joe, are now trainees at City.

49

Manager Jimmy Frizzell had strange ideas on how to please his young charges at Hogmanay 1986. The kilted City boss skirled into the Blues' dressing room ignoring indications from his players that he was tone-deaf! Suffering music-lovers from left to right are Steve Redmond, Paul Moulden, David White, Paul Simpson and Ian Brightwell.

Howard Kendall, who used his knowledge of former players at Goodison to strengthen the City ranks after his appointment, in the same way that Billy McNeill tracked Scottish players after his appointment a few years earlier.

"A ballet good pastime" was the opinion of Brian Horton when he was roped in to participate in the 1994 City pantomime in the Blues' Social Club. Sixteen year old Claire Jackson of the Keating School of Dance in Macclesfield looks somewhat apprehensive that she might find herself in the first team on Saturday!

A smaller than life Alan Ball is interviewed in the tunnel in October 1994. The attendance seems a bit thin, but that's because the sound needed turning up.

Steve Coppell realises how big a club he's taken on, as his concerned expression says...

...while his successor Phil Neal, flanked by German defender Michael Frontzeck, barks out some instructions during a City v Tranmere Rovers game in November 1996. Or else he's joining in the chanting.

Present manager Frank Clark refers to his script to see if things are going according to plan in January 1997. On the other hand, he may be checking the lyrics for a new song he's written to sing on the team bus.

Assistant manager Alan Hill, a long-time friend of Frank Clark, seems perfectly happy with the way things are going...

...while coach Richard Money contemplates innovations for the training pitch now that the Blues are getting things right.

The distinguished-looking Tom Maley who was City's secretary-manager when the Blues won the FA Cup for the first time in 1904. He had built his career with Glasgow Celtic for whom his brother, Willie, also played. Willie had one game for City at his brother's invitation and also turned out minimally for Everton and Manchester United.

The gentleman in the middle is City president Laurence Furniss, an important figure in the Blues' early days. A former player, he became Ardwick's secretary in 1890 and City's chairman in the 1920s. He is pictured in 1934 with the FA Cup that City won after beating Portsmouth. The identity of the shield in unknown and it is thought that the trophy on the left could be the old Lancashire Senior Cup.

The City board in November 1970. Pictured left to right are Sidney Rose (now a City life-president), club secretary Walter Griffiths, chairman Albert Alexander, Frank Johnson, John Humphreys and Eric Alexander, who today is an Honorary President.

Seven months later and some radical changes have taken place. This picture was taken outside Manchester's Midland Hotel and shows left to right Ian Niven, second is an unidentified journalist, then Albert Alexander, Joe Smith and Peter Swales.

The City chairman, president and vice-presidents appear to be deep in rehearsals for a Junior Blues panto! Jazzing it up in front of the old Platt Lane stand are Michael Horwich, Freddy Pye, Peter Swales, Bill Adams and Joe Smith.

A young Franny Lee behaving in the traditional manner of successful young footballers as
the Blues return on an open-topped bus after
winning the 1969 FA Cup final…

…and nearly 30 years later behaving in the
traditional manner of a worried chairman!

Former player Colin Barlow, City's managing direc
tor after Francis Lee had taken over as chairman in
February 1994.

Mike Turner (left), now the Blues' Chief Executive
who joined the club from Liverpool, here seen
watching a City game alongside director David
Bernstein.

It's August 1966 and the Blues are back in the First Division as Second Division champions. Joe Mercer looks quietly satisfied, Malcolm Allison is raring to go, but secretary Walter Griffiths (extreme left) appears not to be very happy with the season ticket sales.

The players who made the most appearances in City's 1968 championship-winning side, together with Malcolm Allison and coach Johnny Hart.

The first-team squad in the 1973-74 season, Denis Law's last one in competitive football. A handsome bunch, even if some of them do seem to have been auditioning for roles in *The Vikings*.

A year later, and this group contains players still involved with Manchester City. Can you pick out Paul Power, Asa Hartford and Peter Barnes?

There are a fair number of international players in this squad for the 1978-79 campaign. Featured with manager Tony Book is Bill Taylor, the England and City coach who sadly died a little later. Now Manchester United's assistant manager, Brian Kidd is third from left on the front row.

No, the Blues didn't take the field a man short. This is the squad for the Soccer Six competition which was held at G-Mex in Manchester in 1987. Neil McNab (front row, extreme right) was the captain.

Featured here is the squad for the Full Members Cup Final against Chelsea in 1986 wearing their Wembley strips. Unhappiest player at the time of the final was defender Kenny Clements (back row, second left) who was badly injured the day before the game in an Old Trafford derby.

Brian Horton's Blues, pictured here before the 1994-95 season began.
Only three seasons have elapsed since this photo was taken and just look at the number of faces no longer with the club.

A typical Frank Swift action shot. Frank first appeared in the League side in 1933-34 and remained with the club until his retirement in 1949. Tragically, this gentle giant was killed in the Munich Air Disaster in 1958 whilst working for a Sunday newspaper.

City were so lucky to have another goal-keeping genius to follow Swift. Bert Trautmann, seen here in action at Maine Road against Arsenal in the 1955-56 season, overcame prejudice and some hostility as a German ex-prisoner-of-war when he signed in 1949. After 545 League and cup appearances for the Blues, over 48,000 people turned up for his testimonial when he retired in 1964.

Joe Corrigan overcame weight problems to develop into yet another excellent keeper for the Blues. He joined the club as a youngster in the late 1960s and gained a total of nine full England caps, a number which would have been far higher had there not been other splendid goalkeepers available at the same time. Here he is seen in action in the 1981 FA Cup Final against Spurs, keeping out an effort from Ossie Ardiles.

When Keith Macrae joined City from Motherwell, the fee of £100,000 was the highest the Blues had ever paid out for a goalkeeper. Strangely he had played at centre-forward for Scotland Boys and had appeared as an outfield player for Motherwell. The improvement in Joe Corrigan's play was such, however, that the red-haired Scot found himself confined to the Reserves for long periods. He climbs high in this picture to hold on to a shot from a Wolves player in the 1974 League Cup Final.

'There was this Englishman, a Welshman and a German…' Seen here training at the Platt Lane Complex are, left to right, £1 million pound signing Tony Coton, now with Sunderland, Martyn Margetson, a former City trainee, and Eike Immel. Eike was forced to retire from the game in 1997 due to a hip injury.

Tommy Wright, City's capture from Nottingham Forest in the spring of 1997. Tommy, a Northern Ireland international, signed for Frank Clark after a loan period with the Blues.

It's easy to forget why goal-keepers are so mollycoddled these days. The following photos from the early '70s show how vicious life was in the box. Here West Brom's John Osborne feels Franny Lee re-arranging his jockstrap while Ian Bowyer makes up the rest of the 'sandwich' in the 1970 League Cup Final...

...then City's Dave Watson puts a loose elbow in another West Brom keeper's solar plexus at The Hawthorns...

...and Wolves' John Richards attempts to pull off City's Keith Macrae's face in the 1974 League Cup Final.

Here it's Kenny Hibbitt's turn in the same game to try to flatten Macrae's Adam's Apple…

…while later in the match Franny Lee appears to be kneeing Gary Pierce in the groin whilst elbowing him in the face.

A right back, Sam Barkas is pictured here practising free-kicks with his left foot. He had won a championship medal with Bradford City in the Third Division North, and with the Blues in Divisions One and Two. He also earned five England caps.

Eric Westwood fluctuated between left-back and outside-left, but eventually settled down in the former position. He had been a Manchester United junior and played for Manchester Boys from the age of 12. In 1944, Eric guested for Chelsea in the War Cup Final against Charlton Athletic,

Welsh international Roy Paul was signed to spearhead City's drive for promotion in 1950-51. On the field, he was a fierce driving force in City's cause, and vowed he would take the Blues back to the Wembley the following year, after their 1954 FA Cup final defeat.

Signed from Southport, Jimmy Meadows eventually found his niche at right-back, and was capped for England. Jimmy's career was cruelly cut short during the 1954 Cup Final when his studs caught in the lush Wembley turf and the wrench badly damaged a knee. Despite a brave attempt at a comeback, in 1961 he was forced to retire and coached and managed teams here and abroad.

'Pull up at Dave's' was a popular saying when Scottish warhorse Dave Ewing was playing at the heart of the City defence. A player with tremendous courage and determination, arguably his finest hour came in the 1956 Cup Final when he protected injured City keeper Bert Trautmann from the Birmingham City forwards.

Mike Doyle began his career at full-back in the youth team. His debut was a quick one: told to pack a bag and head for the airport, he flew to Cardiff, where the Blues were playing on a Friday night in March 1965, as a stand-in for Alan Oakes. Later he found his true position at right-half where he made the bulk of his 558 City appearances.

A strong, brave central defender, Dave Watson was signed from Sunderland in 1975. Sure-footed and quick on the turn, he made life extremely difficult for opposition forwards, and while with City won 30 England caps.

Centre-half Tommy Booth had his own anthem composed by the Kippax fans: 'He's here, he's there, he's every ******* where' during his Maine Road years. His debut was in a League Cup tie at Huddersfield in September 1968, and Joe Mercer was moved to observe that Tommy was 'the best footballing centre-half since Wolves Stan Cullis': praise indeed.

Glasgow Amateurs produced Willie Donachie, who arrived at Maine Road in October 1968. Originally a wing-half, he converted successfully to left-back when injury forced Glyn Pardoe out of the side. Willie was a sure-tackling player who distributed accurately and he went on to appear 426 times in City's first team, scoring two League goals.

Glyn Pardoe holds the record of being City's youngest ever League debutant. He was 15 years and 314 days old when he turned out against Birmingham City in March 1962. Until he finally settled down at left-back, Glyn wore every number except 1 and 5! In 1970, he badly injured a leg in a Manchester derby at Old Trafford, and emergency surgery saved his life. In later years, he coached City's reserve and junior teams.

"He's too old" was Joe Mercer's assessment of Tony Book, then 31, when Malcolm Allison advocated his purchase from Plymouth Argyle. 'Booky' the full-back became one of City's most inspirational skippers, and led the Blues to League and Cup triumphs. Later he took up the managerial reins, his most successful League season being 1976-77 when City were First Division runners-up. He remained with City until part-way through the 1996-97 season.

'Yorkshire grit' is an expression well-suited to the rock-hard Mick McCarthy, a £200,000 buy from Barnsley in 1983. Sure on the ground and powerful in the air, Mick became City's skipper in 1984 but handed the job back to Paul Power. His performances were rewarded with 20 Eire caps while with the Blues. Today he is the Republic's team manager.

Terry Phelan was signed for £2_m from Wimbledon in 1992 and quickly settled down in the left-back position. Already the holder of eight Eire caps, his performances in a sky-blue shirt saw that number grow to 19. He will long be remembered for the goal he scored against Spurs in an FA Cup tie in 1993.

Wimbledon FC just loved Manchester City. Keith Curle was another £2_m signing from the Dons in 1991. The centre-half and City captain also became something of a penalty expert, and is seen here sending the Feyenoord goalkeeper the wrong way in a pre-season friendly in August 1994.

George Heslop was brought in by Joe Mercer in September 1965 to solve the centre-half position, a job he did admirably to assist City out of Division Two in 1966. A member of the First Division championship side in 1968, he remained with City until the early 1970s. He later took over the City Gates, a pub on Hyde Road where Ardwick FC used to change.

Kit Symons was signed by manager Alan Ball from Portsmouth in 1995 and took over the role of City's captain. A Welsh international, Kit made a maximum 38 appearances in his first City season and gained a further five caps for Wales.

Jimmy McMullan was a member of the 'Wembley Wizards', the Scottish side that humiliated England in 1928. Signed by City from Partick Thistle for £4,700 in 1926, this uncle of Matt Busby's was admired for his passing, his reading of the game and his fighting spirit. He played 238 times for the Blues, winning eight of his caps while at Maine Road.

Scorer of City's first goal in the 1956 FA Cup final, Joe Hayes came to City for a trial in 1953, impressed the management, and then asked for his bus fare back to Bolton! He proved to be one of City's most valuable scorers in the '50s and '60s. He topped City's scoring charts twice and was the first post-war player to score 100 goals.

Bobby Johnstone was a tremendously gifted inside-forward who also had an eye for goals. Signed by Les McDowall in Spring 1955, any problems about where Bobby would play in the forward line were solved when Johnny Hart broke a leg at Huddersfield.

Formerly with Hull and Leicester City, Don Revie arrived at Maine Road in 1951. He made his name in 1954-55 when Les McDowall's 'Revie Plan' was named after him, a plan which had been introduced by the successful Hungarian national side. After two Wembley appearances with the Blues, Don joined Sunderland, and later Leeds United where he became manager.

Johnny Crossan was a guiding force behind the Blues' successful promotion bi[...] in 1965-66. An extremely talented inside-forward, he had once been banned for life from playing in the UK because of irregularities concerning an earlier transfer, so he played in Holland. When the ban ended Johnny joined Sunderland, from where Cit[y] signed him. He left City before the 1967-68 season got under way for Middlesbrough. During his career he was capped 24 times by Northern Ireland where he lives today, scouting for Manchester City.

Colin Bell's Bury debut was at Maine Road, when injured City goalkeeper Harry Dowd scored an equaliser as an outfield player. Joe Mercer bought Bell for just £45,000, and he scored on his City debut at Derby. Colin had everything: pace, power, accuracy in passing and shooting, heading, and his stamina earned him the nickname of 'Nijinsky'. He received a bad leg injury after a collision with United's Martin Buchan in a 1975 League Cup tie. After a series of operations and rehabilitation, his comeback was a highly emotional affair, but there was something missing in his play. He won a Central League championship medal in 1978, and later he returned to City as a Youth Development Officer.

'Oh Rodney, Rodney...' The anthem which greeted yet another Rodney Marsh goal in a sky-blue shirt in the 1970s. Bought during City's championship bid in 1971-72, the question of whether he should or should not have been played in the side still remains a controversial one. His impish grin endeared him to the fans, and so did his knack of scoring spectacular goals.

Paul Power is back working for the club he signed for as a teenager in the 1970s, in a revamp of the club's youth policy. Always a fervent Manchester City fan, Paul finished his education before committing himself full-time to the Blues. He settled into mid-field and was later made captain. Probably his finest moment was the goal he scored at Villa Park in 1981 which took the Blues to Wembley. He worked for the Football in the Community programme before his recent appointment at Maine Road.

77

Asa Hartford had two spells with City as a player, the first when he was bought from West Brom in 1974. Manchester City's highest Scottish cap winner moved to Nottingham Forest, and after a spell at Everton he rejoined City in 1981. After coaching and managerial experience with several other clubs, Asa is now on the City coaching staff.

Another Scottish mid-field player, Neil McNab joined the Blues from Brighton, a Billy McNeill signing. Beginning his career with Greenock Morton, Neil moved to Tottenham as a teenager and quickly became known as a terrier of a player who never admitted defeat. He later returned to the Blues where, as a self-confessed City fan, he had three successful years coaching the club's youngsters until 1997.

Paul Lake was a home-grown Blue and a member of the club's FA Youth Cup winning side of 1986. His versatility was instantly recognised. He was, however, embarking on an injury-ridden career. In 1989 he swallowed his tongue in a game against Leicester City, then against Aston Villa in 1990 he severely damaged his cruciate ligament. In 1991, the knee broke down again at Middlesbrough. After 16 operations Paul finally had to admit defeat and he retired in January 1996. His successful testimonial match against Manchester United in October 1997 brought deserved financial rewards, and his wife gave birth on the same day.

Steve Lomas - seen here celebrating a goal against Nottingham Forest - came to City as a trainee in 1990 and rose to gain first team status in 1993. His wholehearted approach to the game plus his fiery temperament made him a fans' favourite, and Northern Ireland recognised his skills by awarding him his first senior cap in 1994 against Romania. He was transferred to West Ham in 1997.

Manchester City were without a manager when the opportunity arose to sign Georgian Georgiou Kinkladze from Dynamo Tbilisi in 1995, so City chairman Francis Lee seized the initiative and secured the player's signature. Here he is seen signing for City at the chairman's Wilmslow home with club secretary Bernard Halford also looking pleased with the capture.

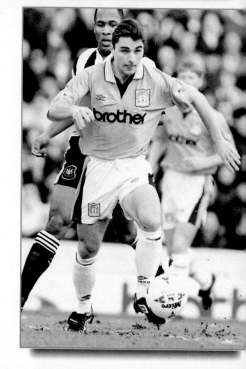

Although short, the Georgian international possesses mercurial skills, and has become the target of serious man-to-man marking, particularly in away games. Some of his goals have become City classics, such as the one against Southampton in an FA Cup tie, and he can be deadly in free-kick situations. Ask Swindon Town's Fraser Digby!

Former Welsh miner Billy Meredith soon built himself up as one of the most graceful and dangerous wingers of the early 20th century. At City, he was the leading scorer in four seasons, and won 22 of his 48 caps. In 1905 he was banned for a season for offering a bribe to an Aston Villa defender. It emerged in an inquiry that the City management had been paying illegal high wages and bonuses. Draconian sentences were passed, and Meredith was transferred to Manchester United. He guested for City during World War One, then re-signed for the Blues in 1921. He finally hung up his boots in 1924.

Eric Brook came from Barnsley along with Freddy Tilson, and he had a habit of popping up in various forward positions. 'Brooky' kept a firm grip on the No.11 shirt, and was capped by England 18 times. A car crash on his way to a wartime international fixture ended his career, and he retired after appearing in 491 City League and cup games and scoring 177 goals.

Three consecutive League games in three different divisions is former City left-winger Roy Clarke's proud record. He moved from Cardiff City (Third Division South) to the Blues, played in the last game in the Second Division in June 1947, then opened his First Division career in 1947-48 campaign. Apart from a short spell in the late '50's/early '60s, Roy has been associated with the Blues for six decades, as player, social club manager, and now with the Former Players Association.

Controversy and Tony Coleman were never away. A player who had once been suspended *sine die* for a fracas with a referee, he cost Joe Mercer only £12,000 in 1967, but brought balance to the front line. His attitude to full-backs was uncompromising. The Coleman stories became cameos: there were the tattoos to be removed before he met the Princess Royal at Wembley, there was the (alleged) punch-up with Malcolm Allison in a Manchester night-club after curfew time, and so on. He eventually went to Sheffield Wednesday, Blackpool and a number of other clubs before retirement.

Mike Summerbee was the second Mercer signing in 1965 from Swindon Town. He performed at first in the middle of the front line, but when Francis Lee arrived in 1967, he tormented defenders from the wing. Mike was capped eight times for England after 1968. He turned out in 427 games for the Blues before joining Burnley. Today he is involved in City's commercial activities.

Part of Sunderland's FA Cup winning side of 1973, Dennis Tueart joined City with colleague Mick Horswill. His debut was in a bad-tempered derby game at Maine Road. He scored a number of excellent hat-tricks during his City career, but will best be remembered for the overhead kick in the 1976 League Cup Final which brought the winning goal. He played alongside some of the world's greatest footballers at New York Cosmos, but returned to Maine Road in January 1980. At City. he played 269 games in all and he scored 107 times, an excellent record for a winger.

Son of former star Ken Barnes, Peter joined City from school and his skills helped him to rise through the junior ranks into the reserve side and then the first team. He won the Young Footballer of the Year award in 1976 having scored a Wembley goal the day before. He was sold to West Brom, as was his friend Gary Owen, in 1979, and he then played for a succession of clubs both at home and abroad.

'And it *is* ten!' screamed the TV commentator as David White slammed home City's 10th goal (and his hat-trick) in the 10-1 rout of Huddersfield Town in November 1987. Another member of City's 1986 youth side, David was never afraid to try his luck against the keeper, and he registered 95 League and cup goals in 333 outings, including a four in a game at Villa Park. He gained one England cap while with City.

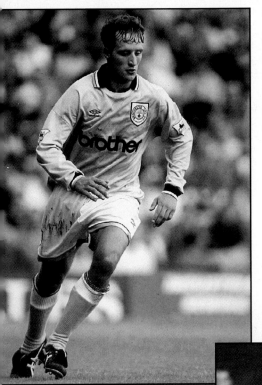

Like his father, Mike, Nicky Summerbee joined City from Swindon Town, and there were questions as to which was his best position. Against the Blues he had always played well as a full-back, but he showed up well when going full speed at a defender and getting the ball across from the bye-line. He is always capable of cutting inside and letting loose a shot.

Peter Beagrie was signed by Brian Horton in March 1994 in a successful attempt to lift the Blues to Premiership safety. A skilful and tricky winger, his trademark was a double back-flip when he scored a goal. However, a large part of his City career disappeared because of injury and tendonitis, and he was transferred to Bradford City in the summer of 1997.

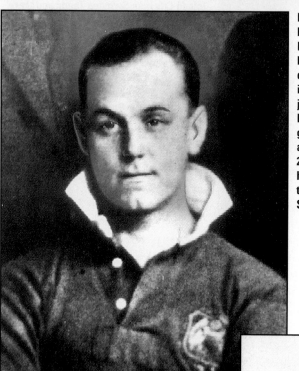

Freddy Tilson, the 1934 Cup Final hero, the man who told his City colleagues in the dressing-room at half-time with the Blues a goal down: 'Doan't worry, Ah'll bang two in in th' second 'alf!" And he did just that. He was signed from Barnsley (along with Eric Brook): goals flowed from his lethal boots, and at City he scored 132 times in 273 outings. After World War Two, he returned to City as the reserve team trainer and later became Chief Scout.

Peter Doherty, a record City signing from Blackpool in 1936, with a host of clubs also after his signature. During City's championship season of 1937-38, Peter was leading scorer with 30 goals. He left City in unhappy circumstances in 1945 to join Derby County, and later played for Huddersfield Town. His managerial career included Doncaster Rovers and Northern Ireland.

A splendidly typical action shot of Francis Lee as he sends the ball thundering goalwards in a Maine Road League game. A £65,000 arrival from Bolton Wanderers in 1967, his goals did so much to bring a whole succession of silver cups and trophies to City, while his collection of England caps rose to 27. He created a City record by scoring 15 penalties in all competitions in the 1971-72 season, and was dubbed Lee One Pen by the media. Franny was sold surprisingly to Derby County in 1974, scored for them at Maine Road, and won a Championship medal!

This fine action shot of Wyn 'The Leap' Davies was taken during a League game against Leeds United at Maine Road. Wyn had featured in the same Bolton Wanderers side as Franny Lee and the Blues signed him from Newcastle United in 1971. Always one of the first names to be pencilled in on the Wales team sheet, Wyn gained a total of 34 caps. He became one of the few post-war players to play for both City and Manchester United.

Denis Law cost City £55,000 when Les McDowall signed him in March 1960, A.C.Torino almost doubling that fee in 1961. Matt Busby later bought him for Manchester United. He was given a free transfer by United in 1973 and he rejoined City for just one season, contributing to the downfall of United in 1974. Denis had extremely quick reflexes and was lethal in the penalty area, putting balls into the net which other forwards might have given up on. Here he is blasting a shot through the Walsall defence in a League Cup tie at Maine Road.

One of City's first apprentices, Neil Young spent the early part of his career on the right wing for the Blues, but Joe Mercer made him more of a striker in the No.10 shirt. A tall and always elegant player, Neil topped the City scoring charts in three seasons, and of course it was his excellent goal which brought the FA Cup to Manchester in 1969. In January 1972, he moved to Preston North End and today runs successful soccer schools.

These three might well smile! They've just scored a hat-trick apiece against Huddersfield Town in a 10-1 win in November 1987. Paul Stewart (left) was formerly with Blackpool, and joined the Blues in March 1987: his form caused Tottenham Hotspur to fork out £1.7m for him in the summer of 1988. Tony Adcock (right) was to score another hat-trick a few days later against Plymouth Argyle in the Simod Cup competition. For David White (centre), see 'Wicked Wingers'. Oh, and let's not forget the scorer of the opening goal: mid-field maestro Neil McNab.

Republic of Ireland international Niall Quinn was languishing in Arsenal's reserves when Howard Kendall signed him, and he scored on his City League debut against Chelsea. His height made him a very difficult opponent, and he was surprisingly nimble in the penalty area. He scored a 'classic hat-trick' against Crystal Palace at Selhurst Park in 1991, left and right feet and a header as well! Niall moved to Sunderland in 1996 having scored 76 goals in 241 games for City: he had the decency to apologise to City fans for the team being relegated that year. Cruciate ligament injuries have dogged his later years.

Few became fans' favourites in as short a space of time as these two players. Paul Walsh joined City from Portsmouth in March 1994 and became an instant success in a City side which began to play some very attractive football. The 'little genius' pulled opposition defences inside out with his darting runs and close control, and a display against one of his former clubs, Spurs, will long be savoured by those who saw it. Paul returned to Portsmouth in 1995, but suffered a cruciate ligament injury shortly afterwards.

'Oo-vay! Oo-vay!' The roar that signalled yet another Uwe Rösler goal. The popular German striker came on trial from FC Nurnberg in 1994 and scored two goals in his first City appearance, a reserve game against Burnley. He repeated his goal-scoring feats in the first team, scoring 22 times in his first full season. He was later joined by another colourful German character, Maurizio Gaudino. In the autumn of 1997, Uwe was placed on the transfer list when he refused the terms of a new contract.

The date was 27th March 1920, and here is the City team being introduced to His Majesty King George V at Hyde Road. The match between the Blues and Liverpool was the first one attended by royalty outside London. Max Woosnam can be seen (third from left) and the trainer on the extreme right is Jimmy Broad. The main stand in the background was destroyed by fire on November 1920. And the result? It was 2-1, Horace Barnes scoring twice for the Blues.

Yet another distinguished visitor to the Hyde Road ground, this time Prime Minister A.J.Balfour, chatting before the game to City winger Billy Meredith, accompanied by two City officials. The date was 29thSeptember 1900 and the result against Stoke was 2-0 to City. The gentleman on the left in the natty jacket and cap is the referee.

Joe Mercer contemplates the pitch from the corner of the main stand and the old Scoreboard end, being demolished in the 1971-72 season to make way for the new North Stand. Here the removal of the advertising hoardings has begun, while a man with a power tool attacks one of the iron crush barriers. When the North Stand, was finished all four sides of the ground were covered.

An institution disappears. It's 1994 and the Kippax Stand, home to millions of spectators since 1923, falls to the bulldozer and pneumatic drill. The North Stand can be seen behind Head Groundsman Stan Gibson, who appears to be indicating what might happen to someone should any rubble land on his sacred turf.

The new Kippax Stand under construction and seen from an unusual angle. It dwarfs the rows of neat, well-cared for terrace houses, and is having seats installed in the middle tier. Note the budding young Blues in the street hoping to catch the attention of a City scout.

Hold on, nobody's pinched the goal-posts and replaced them, and there *aren't* too many players on the pitch. This was the first Rugby League game at Maine Road for 30 years, between Oldham and Featherstone Rovers in January 1987. Happily the fencing is now gone and so is the former Platt Lane Stand, replaced by seating and executive boxes. The football goal-posts are visible in the far left hand corner.

This shot of the Official Entrance to Maine Road was taken in the early 1960s. Since then the whole facade of the main stand has been redesigned, with two curving staircases inside the front door replacing the straight flight of stairs that can be seen here. How long it would take today's posties to push the mail through that letter-box!

It's 1982 and the main stand is getting a new roof. Gone is the traditional sloping cover with the pillars which impeded spectators' views, and instead this new curving cantilever roof was installed. It was originally intended to have executive boxes overlooking the pitch, but these were shelved due to the expense.

It's a Manchester City photocall in August 1990 and Colin Hendry inspects the Blues as they cross the pitch in front of the old Platt Lane Stand. That imposing edifice of scaffolding was a stage under construction for one of the famous Maine Road rock concerts held during the 1990s. Top acts included Queen, Dire Straits, The Rolling Stones, David Bowie, Jean Michel Jarre and Oasis.

Maine Road 1997

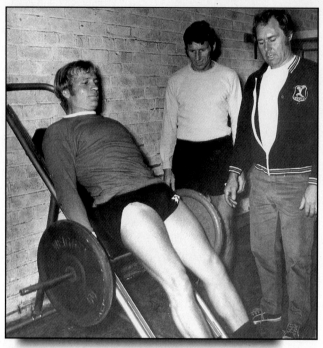

August 1970 and Franny Lee - showing an alarming amount thigh! - tests a new weight training machine presented to the Blues by a friend of Tony Book's, Tony Horler, a Somerse gymnasium proprietor...

...and three years later furthe progress was made to help the players achieve maximum fitness when a £1,400 Multigym was introduced. On it, 14 players could work simultaneousl or 28 players working in partnership. Under the eye of a pa of visitors, one of the club's young hopefuls, Willie Donachie, aims to develop the arm muscles to improve his throw-ins. Behind Willie, Rodney Marsh does his best to stop the wall from collapsing.

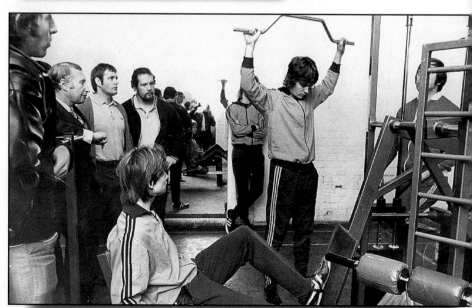

Two indispensable City background workers in the 1970s. Like all good mums, Anne Nightingale and Joyce Johnstone insisted that their lads were turned out properly, and washed 50 shirts a day, plus training gear, shorts, socks and towels.

From the same period, here is a shot of some of the 'Mrs Mopps' of Maine Road, the cleaning ladies together with club steward Ron Shawcross. Left to right are head cleaner Mary May, Marilyn Durston, Doris White (all of Fallowfield) and Flo Palin from Moss Side.

The David Bowie concerts are over and here Head Groundsman Stan Gibson (retired 1997) grits his teeth as he examines the damage done to the pitch by the hordes of fans on the two nights. Although boards were laid down, the sheer weight of numbers pressed them into the turf. It was a good job there was plenty of time for its recovery before the new season.

Carrying the trainer's bag, the figure on the left is club doctor Norman Luft who is accompanying Paul Lake after he swallowed his tongue in a match against Leicester City in March 1989.

It's quite impossible to calculate the value of the work this trio has put into Manchester City. Johnny Hart (left) was player, coach and manager, having joined the club during World War Two. When Harry Godwin (centre) was Chief Scout, he continually brought a rich vein of young talent into the club, as did Ken Barnes (right) when he took over the role. Ken's playing career saw him captain the Blues at one stage.

Crowd safety is of paramount importance on match days, and in recent years more and more stewards, many of them radio-linked, are used rather than the police. Here City's Safety Officer, Jack Richards, goes over last-minute plans with some senior stewards, while a small number of policemen await kick-off.

For pre-season training, the Blues often get away from the Platt Lane training complex, and in the past have used Wythenshawe Park and the University playing fields. Here bespectacled athlete Danny Herman leads a group round the track at Longford Park, Stretford. The players include Mike Summerbee, Tony Book, and Derek Jeffries.

The Platt Lane training complex prior to its development into the Oasis restaurant and improved changing facilities...

...and this is the 200-seater restaurant (upper storey) overlooking a group of youngsters from the local community. The improvements cost £1.5m with the help of the Manchester city council and contain a fully-equipped physiotherapy suite.

The Astrodome at Platt Lane is seen here well under way. The completion date is in April 1998, and it will house all sorts of inside sports and leisure pursuits, open to the local community with whom City have built up an excellent relationship.

The old Manchester City Souvenir Shop at Maine Road, adjoining the Social Club. Its limited space led to both buildings being converted into the City Megastore early in the 1997-98 season.

Another outlet for City merchandise, opened in the Arndale Centre in the heart of the city. Here an eager crowd of Blues await the official opening performed by City players.

1

FINAL TIE
of the
Football Association
Challenge Cup
Competition

OFFICIAL
SOUVENIR
PROGRAMME
6ᴰ

EMPIRE STADIUM ⁕ WEMBLEY
APRIL 29ᵗʰ 1933

| BEST PICTURES | EXPERT CRITICISM OF TO-DAY'S CUP TIE BY CHARLES BUCHAN *(the famous International and ex-Arsenal Captain)* | ON MONDAY |

News ⁕⁕ Chronicle

PRINTED & PUBLISHED BY F. E. BLOWER & CO. SUTTON RD WORKS. WATFORD.

2

29. APRIL 1970
EUROPACUP-FINALSPIEL
DER POKALSIEGER

MANCHESTER CITY – GORNIK-ZABRZE

HERAUSGEGEBEN
VOM ÖSTERREICHISCHEN FUSSBALL-BUND
IM AUFTRAG DER U.E.F.A.

1) 1933. King George V was on the throne and the Official Cup Final programme, sponsored by the *News Chronicle* daily newspaper, cost 6d (2.5p). Everton beat City 3-0. Note that the teams' names were absent from the cover.

2) Clearly for students of German, this programme was issued for the European Cup-Winner's Cup Final in the Prater Stadium, Vienna. The history of MCFC begins: 'Ursprünglich als West Gorton und später als Ardwick bekannt, wurde der Klub unter lezterem Namen Mitglied der Football Alliance im Jahre 1891'. It gets harder after that.

3) More silverware on the way. City faced up to Newcastle United and beat them 2-1 in the 1976 League Cup Final, thanks to goals from Peter Barnes and Dennis Tueart. Now both teams are in glorious technicolour on the front page. Today's fan would have to shell out far more than 20p for a similar programme.

4) We've progressed to the team names on the cover. Bert Trautmann was the luckiest man alive - literally - at the end of this Cup Final. Not only did he have a winner's medal but he had survived playing the latter stages of the game with a broken neck. The Manchester Blues won 3-1. The referee, Alf Bond, only had one arm. Did he ask players to book themselves with his pencil and notebook?

3

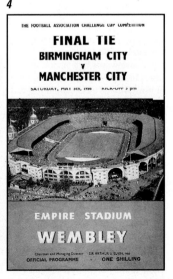

MANCHESTER CITY

SATURDAY, 28th FEBRUARY 1976 · Kick-off 3.30 pm

THE FOOTBALL LEAGUE

CUP FINAL

WEMBLEY STADIUM

Official Souvenir Programme . . . . Twenty pence

NEWCASTLE UNITED

4

THE FOOTBALL ASSOCIATION CHALLENGE CUP COMPETITION

FINAL TIE
BIRMINGHAM CITY
V
MANCHESTER CITY

SATURDAY, MAY 5th, 1956 · KICK-OFF 3 pm

EMPIRE STADIUM
WEMBLEY

Chairman and Managing Director SIR ARTHUR J. ELVIN, MBE
OFFICIAL PROGRAMME - ONE SHILLING

1

2

1) The original title of the City programme was the 'Blue and White', and this one was issued for a fourth round FA Cup replay against Swindon Town at Maine Road in January 1930. The Blues romped home 10-1, the scorers being Marshall 5, Tait 3, Johnson and Brook. An advert informs the reader that he could buy a made-to-measure suit for 45 shillings (£2.25p)! Volant, incidentally, was a *nom de plume*, a practice then quite common.

2) What a far cry from the glossy magazines we're used to these days! Paper was rationed during World War Two, so for much of the war a single sheet was issued. It did however contain a consider-able amount of club news on the reverse side. Clubs quite often had no idea what their line-up would be right up to kick-off, and it wasn't uncom-mon to ask for volunteer play-ers from the crowd. Note the sponsor: Hydes Pale Ale.

3) By the time this derby match was played just after Christmas 1957, City had abandoned manager Les McDowall's latest plan. In fact it had lasted only two games, the Blues losing 1-6 at Preston and 2-9 at West Brom. These scorelines helped the club into the record books that season when they scored 104 goals and conceded 100. The ground looks nothing like '50s Maine Road, especially with-out the floodlights!

4) The Blues returned to the First Division. Wolves were the visitors and the result was 0-0. Skipper Roy Paul missed a penalty. The 'Stone-Dri' advert on the cover was one associated with City for many years. For younger readers, 2d is less than 1p!

3

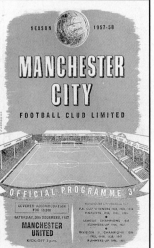

4

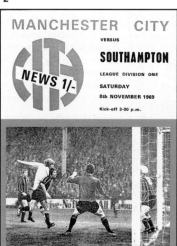

1) A new season and a new division! The cover shows a different aerial view of Maine Road. City's first home game in the 1966-67 season was against Liverpool and the Blues showed off the Second Division championship trophy before the game.

2) What a hectic season this one was for Manchester City, involved in two major cup competitions right up to the final of each! The programme is called 'City News' and action shots are normal now. On the back of this programme you could win £100 (or £3800 in today's money) in a free 'Scoreboard Scoop' competition.

Normally the FA Charity ield is contested by the ague winners and FA p victors, but this one in 73 was by invitation hen City met Burnley. It as my wife's birthday t nobody told City, Colin ll's future business rtner Colin Waldron ing allowed to score e only goal of the game r the visitors. What a esent! This was the first me the words 'Match agazine' appeared on e cover, and by now we ere 'decimal'.

The cover here depicts e League Championship phy which the Blues on in 1968 for only the cond time in their histo- The result of this match as 1-1. The design was artistic step forward ith the silhouetted foot- ller.

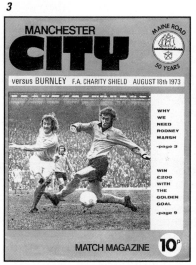

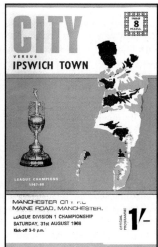

1

1) Not a World War Two Casualty Clearing Station, but Roy Bailey's treatment room at Maine Road. Roy is treating Tommy Booth's thigh. This programme was for the opening game of the season when City drew with Arsenal, Brian Kidd our scorer in a 1-1 draw. Malcolm Macdonald scored for the Gunners. There is an excellent report on the second Junior Blues rally at Belle Vue in this first landscape Magazine.

2

3) The first home programme of the 1976-77 campaign which contained a farewell to Alan Oakes, welcomes to Brian Kidd and chief coach Bill Taylor, and news that the Blues were to face Juventus in the UEFA Cup. This is the first home Match Magazine cover to be printed in colour (a bit fuzzy, sadly).

2) City celebrated this historic photo - complete with laundry basket but minus Stan Gibson's cat! - taken on the Maine Road forecourt with a splendid 4-2 victory over Norwich City. As far as is known this is the first picture of all the club's employees, management and directors that was taken, with Peter Swales at the apex. Also, dig the '70s typeface!

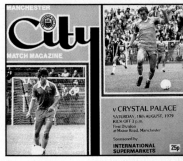

4) A new campaign that failed to live up to Malcolm Allison's expectations. He brought in four newcomers in the summer of 1979 - Dragoslav Stepanovic, Michael Robinson, Bobby Shinton and Steve MacKenzie - for well over £1,446,000. Dave Watson, Peter Barnes, and Asa Hartford all left. The match sponsors were International Supermarkets. Another 'crazee' '70s logo.

1

Barclays League Division Two
Saturday, 5th September, 1987
CITY v. BLACKBURN ROVERS
Kick-Off 3.00 p.m.

2

ARSENAL

2) Tommy Caton adorns the front cover, in a porthole picture. This was the one season when England star Trevor Francis played for Manchester City, getting off to a super start with a brace of goals away at Stoke City. He didn't score in this game against Arsenal. The following season's ticket prices are included in this issue; it would cost £25 to stand on the Kippax, without discount.

1) A Second Division game which was defender Kenny Clements' 200th City League game. The cover shows Paul Stewart, Imre Varadi and Paul Simpson in celebratory mood. Here the design changed back to a vertical format. Sponsors Brother make their debut.

4) The opening programme of the 1984-85 season at the end of which the Blues were promoted. Philips have replaced Saab as the club's sponsors and the match itself was multi-sponsored. The two players shown are new signings David Phillips and Tony Cunningham.

3) Two new Scots at the helm and three new Scots on the books. Recently appointed manager Billy McNeill dresses up his number two, Jimmy Frizzell, in City gear ready for the new season when the Blues hoped for promotion. The three Scottish players brought in were Neil McNab, Jim Tolmie and Derek Parlane. It was the club's second season with sponsors Saab (1983): the Magazine was reduced in size and pagination.

4

1

2

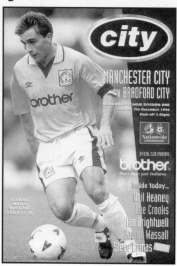

1) Right up to date with this one, including high quality photos and state-of-the-art design! A cove from the current season, the main photo is an act shot of Dutchman Gerar Wiekens. City's new coa of-arms adorns the uppe right-hand corner.

2) Geo Kinkladze graces the cover of this edition, game against Bradford C in 1996. Note the price - £1.70 - and the plethora advertisers' and sponsor logos.

3) City v Queens Park Rangers in 1991 was the Blues' 4000th competitive game since the club joined the Football League as Ardwick in 1892. The result was 2-2. The magazine - which it was rather than a programme - appears now in a larger format.

4) Clearly Uwe Rösler was 'up for it' as the Blues faced up to Feyenoord from Rotterdam in a pre-season friendly in 1994. The result however showed that the Blues were not quite ready for Europe. It's interesting to see how much modern technology enhances the cover, and the size has increased to 48 pages.

3

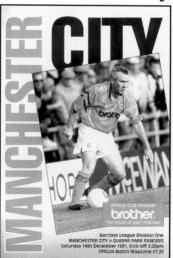

4

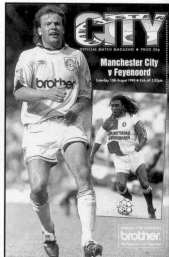

Manor Park Technical Grammar School, Newcastle-on-Tyne, and the end of the 1961-62 season. Featured on this team shot (front row, second from left) is 12-year-old Dennis Tueart, who, we have learned, was also a useful cricketer...

...and here is future Blue full-back Willie Donachie, seen here with the rest of his class at a Glasgow junior school. Our bet is that Willie is on the back row, third from left.

The Whitley brothers, Jeff
(left) and Jim, seem happy
enough as they contem-
plate their future with City.
Zambian-born, Jeff has
logically been capped by
Northern Ireland and has
broken through into City's
first team, while Jim has
shown a great deal of
promise in the reserve
side.

The brothers Brightwell,
the footballing ones,
change sports and partake
in the Manchester City
Golf Classic to raise funds
for the Youth Development
programme at Maine Road.
Contrary to all pen-por-
traits of Ian (left) and David
(second from right), we
have absolutely no idea
who their 'famous athlete
parents are!

Former City Chief Scout Ken Barnes here toasts the selection of son Peter for the England squad in 1977 against Italy. Ken was once an England reserve and played for the Football League and various FA teams, and he is clearly delighted with the progress Peter has made.

You can read about Paul Lake elsewhere in this book, but how many people know that brother Mike (right) had trials in City's Reserves? He had six games back in 1985-86, and although Mike wasn't taken on at Maine Road, he did play League football for Sheffield United and Wrexham.

111

Here Darren (left) and Jason Beckford are seen autographing postcards at a Stockport travel agent's in aid of Comic Relief. Darren was a prolific scorer in the Blues' junior sides, at one time scoring hat-tricks for fun it seemed, while Jason - now working in the Football in the Community programme at Maine Road - was a mid-fielder who also had an eye for goals.

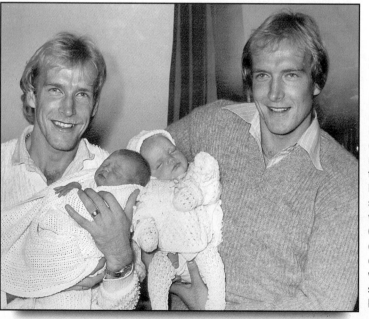

It must have been the Manchester air! The Futcher twins not only joined City at roughly the same time in 1978, but they became dads just seven weeks apart a year later! Here Paul (left) shows off daughter Melanie, only a few hours old, while Ron clutches sleeping partner Nicola Melanie.

Gary Owen gets his marching orders in an UEFA Cup tie against Standard Liege in Belgium in 1978. He had remonstrated forcibly with Philippe Garot who had committed a foul on Asa Hartford. However, the Blues overcame their opponents over the two legs, 4-2.

Aage Hareide arrived from Molde FK in Norway in October 1981. His appearances for the Blues were limited, although he did win nine Norwegian caps while with City. He moved on to Norwich City and then returned home. Today he is a manager for Volvo

In action here is Kaziu Deyna, signed from Polish Army side Legia Warsaw. The game was a UEFA Cup tie against Borussia Munchengladbach ('Give us a B...'), Kazi came on as a substitute and scored, but City lost 3-1. The Pole, capped 102 times by his country, was a free-kick expert and scored some exquisite goals. Sadly he was killed in a car crash in California after leaving City to coach in the USA.

Kaare Ingebrigtsen, another Norwegian, came from Rosenborg in January 1993 where he been involved in no less than three League and cup doubles. He appeared 17 times for City, 11 of those as a sub, before returning home on loan in the summer. His moment of Blue glory came with a hat-trick against Leicester City in an FA Cup tie at Maine Road in January 1994.

Another action shot from the Borussia game. City's Nicky Reid made his first senior appearance, included in the side to mark European Footballer of the Year Allan Simonsen. Nicky's fine performance led to his League debut for the Blues at Ipswich three weeks later.

A tall, brave player, Dutchman Michel Vonk quickly became a fans' favourite at Maine Road. He arrived from Dordrecht in March 1992 and in all played 103 games, scoring six times. It was clear that he would drop in the pecking order with the signing of Kit Symons, so after a loan period with Oldham Athletic, Michel moved to Sheffield United.

A close shave! City were drawn against Linfield from Northern Ireland in this Cup Winner's Cup tie in September 1970. A late goal from Colin Bell gave the Blues a 1-0 lead in the first leg, but the City team had the shock of their lives when Linfield won 2-1 in Belfast. This goal by Franny Lee gave the Blues a win under the away goals rule, and they went on to reach the semi-finals when they were beaten by Chelsea.

Former Ajax player Alphonse Groenendijk ('There's only one Alphonse...') maintained that he enjoyed his spell with City, but like some other European players he found the pace of the game quite different to what he had been used to back home. 'Fonz' turned out in only 12 games after his arrival in July 1993 and later returned to Holland to play for Sparta Rotterdam.

This European Cup tie against Turkish champions Fenerbahce was City's first venture into European competition in September 1968. Despite coach Malcolm Allison's statements about terrifying continental sides, the first leg's goalless result was a great disappointment, and the Blues lost the second leg 2-1. Tony Coleman became the first Blue to score in a Euro competition.

A flamboyant figure with his designer stubble and flowing locks, Maurizio Gaudino - German in spite of the Italian-sounding name - joined City on loan in December 1994 from Eintracht Frankfurt, where he had had a dispute with the coach. He slotted into the team easily and scored four goals in 25 appearances. Returning to Germany the following summer, he found the Polizei awaiting him to chat about alleged car fraud.

One of City's finest hours! This UEFA Cup tie in the San Siro stadium had been delayed 24 hours due to fog, but there was nothing foggy about the Blues' performance as they drew 2-2 with AC Milan, winning overall 5-2. Both home and away displays were excellent, the goals in Italy coming from a Brian Kidd header and a shot from Paul Power, who had run 70 yards with the ball and beat two defenders in front of goal.

Obviously these two foreign stars need no introduction. Uwe's bow is in recognition of Geo's skills after the Georgian had threaded his way through a packed opposition defence before laying on a simple chance for the German. The goal was against Southend United in February 1997.

City's youth side in a jubilant mood after beating Manchester United in the Lancashire Youth Cup final in May 1983 to retain the trophy. Previous City scalps had been Bolton (3-1) and Burnley (6-0). The Blues won this final 2-1 at Old Trafford thanks to Paul Simpson's two goals.

Back in July 1968, the City youngsters begin pre-season training with a gentle stroll around the pitch at Maine Road. The new apprentices that summer were Mike Brennan, Steve Carter, Ronnie Healey (all of whom later played for the first team), Stuart Curtin and Les Milner.

In 1986-87, the Reserves won the Central League championship for only the second time since the competition started 1911. All the player this photograph ha either played in the first team or would so. Back row left to right are leading sc er Jason Beckford, Ian Scott, Paul Lake Ian Brightwell, Ear Barrett and Andy Hinchcliffe. The fro row is Paul Moulde Paul Simpson, Stev Redmond and Davi White.

The lad with his hands proudly on the Manchester County Trophy in 1961-62 is none other than John Clay, a City player in the '60s and now the Blues' Public Relations Officer. The team was Stockport Boys and the other 'smiler' is Mike Doyle.

Having broken through into the first team in 1996-97, here are Chris Greenacre (left) and Lee Crooks, both from Wakefield, as they sign Associated Schoolboy forms at the age of 14 under the watchful eye of former Youth Development Officer Terry Farrell.

The 1992 City youth squad. This was the season they won the Lancashire Youth Cup, beating Preston North End 4-0 at Deepdale. Scorers were Nicky Limber, Adie Mike, and subs Rae Ingram and Nevin Riches.

We go right back to the 1950s for this shot. It's the youth side who were beaten 0-4 by Manchester United in the third round of the FA Youth Cup at Maine Road on 15th December 1958. Future first-teamer David Wagstaffe is second from the left on the back row, with Alan Oakes second from the right. Another, David Shawcross, is in the middle of the front row.

Chief Scout Harry Godwin's prowess at spotting a 'good 'un' is legendary, and here is yet another capture. Being handed over by Harry to trainer Johnny Hart is Peter Barnes, with father Ken happily looking on.

A very youthful and apprehensive look-ing Colin Bell not long after he travelled down to Bury to join the Shakers from his native County Durham. His debut at Maine Road for them would bring him a goal, and his record with the Blues betrayed no sign of nerves whatsoever!

This section began with a Lancashire Youth Cup win for City and here's anoth-er! This time the victims were Bolton Wanderers in April 1984, and the score was 3-0 with Darren Beckford, Ian Scott and Steve Redmond on target.

Looking like extras f
The Untouchables, h
are ten elegant mem
of the City side who
just won the League
championship in 193
celebrating by tourir
Hitler's Germany. The
players who have lo
their waistcoats are
Peter Doherty, Bobby
Marshall and (partly
den) Jack Bray, whil
those who are sarto
correct are Alec Her
Ernie Toseland, Billy
Dale, Frank Swift, Er
Brook, Sam Barkas a
Freddy Tilson. Hands
pockets was compul

Nearly 40 years later
here the 1976 League
squad, with boss Ton
Book, show that they
only have a flare for
ball but a flare for
trousers as well! The
lapels, the tie knots a
the shirt collars are a
wide as the hair cuts
With Tueart's strides
length there should b
need to employ a sw
er-up at Maine Road.

Tycoon-to-be Franny Lee in his Bolton Wanderers days checks his waste-paper collection for press-cuttings to go in his scrapbook before the pulper starts work. Note the drainpipe trousers, the Beatles fringe and the small knot on the tie…

…while by the time he signed for Derby County in 1974 after seven years with City, he could obviously splash out in dazzling fashion. Whether the photographer here wore sunglasses isn't recorded, but Franny's gear included a loud, loud check and '70s 'paisley' patterned shirt with penny-collars. Also a chunky bracelet and a chunky haircut.

Still sporting the flares and high-waisted Oxford Bags, and with shirt collars like seagulls' wings, here are City and England stars Dennis Tueart and Dave Watson pictured with a young fan at a Variety Club Sponsored Walk at Maine Road in 1975. Somebody in the Tueart and Watson households has clearly been busy with the knitting needles as the skinny-ribbed tanktop pullovers testify. By the way, if the young man on the bike is *you*, why the bike?

Ready to take the capital by storm, the ladies practising their Tiller Girls routine are the wives, fiancées and girl-friends of the Blues' 1976 League Cup squad. They are all very smartly turned out in midis, trouser suits and skinny-rib tops, yet there are widely differing individual tastes. Marie Bell and Penny Watson fear the cold in the metropolis and have gone for high boots, while Sue Barrett and Yvonne Donachie think it's warm enough for sandals. Local hairdressers have clearly been busy too!

Back to the 1930s, and trying in vain to autograph a leather ball with a fountain pen is City winger Eric Brook. Turn-ups on the trousers are *de rigeur*, while the player with the newspaper under his arm appears to have lost his belt and braces! The politically incorrect lady in the fox fur is responding to another player's request as to where she bought that charming hat. Note Matt Busby's razor sharp centre-parting, while Frank Swift parts to the right.

Billy McNeill is now manager and the Blues are off on a pre-season tour of Germany. Hipsters are in, with only a modest flare, thin lapels and ties abound, and everybody looks like they're off to a disco in Hale. Neil McNab (on tarmac, third from right) feels that this outfit 'suits' him, and Jim Tolmie (next to Neil) and Tommy Caton (third from left) still favour tight perms. And what about those white slip-on shoes, sported by Graham Baker and Steve Kinsey? Note too the wide taste in tabloids.

18-year-old Greta Foster, the Blues' 1976 Miss Manchester City. From Salford, free-lance go-go dancer Greta had been a City fan all her life. With all that metal on the costume and the identity dogtags around the neck, Greta didn't go out in a thunder-storm!

Two years on and now it was the turn of 19-year-old Janet Crewdson to wear the crown. Much more conservatively dressed, Janet favoured a swept-back pageboy hairstyle, a velvet jacket and open-toed sandals.

Here's Janet again after her term of office, handing over the winner's rosebowl to 24-year-old receptionist Mary Campbell from Shaw, near Oldham. The Marilyn Monroe lookalike also received a cheque, a silver bracelet, a bottle of bubbly and a bouquet.

Giving the budgie a close-up of her charms, here is the 1982 Manchester City Queen decorating an already very decorative settee. It's hairdresser Lynn Mountain, a former model, from Withington. Naturally her fiancé, Philip Bates, was also a City-supporting hairdresser.

Two years on and it's blond beauty Ellen Hanlon who is working out on the club's multi-trainer in the gym. Ellen is preparing for the Manchester City 10K and Fun Run in October 1984, and although she looks very fit indeed, maybe dragging that machine around after her could prove too great a handicap.

No compilation of City photographs would be complete without Helen Turner and her famous bell. Preparing here to follow the Blues to who-knows-where, she shows off a saucy garter for the benefit of the cameraman. She was once told that the bell was an offensive weapon; those who sat near her agreed!

The Blues can boast fans all over the world and the Norwegian branch has always been a particularly strong one. Here is a party in 1977 who have just arrived at Manchester Airport to see City
play Arsenal at Maine Road in February 1977. One thing puzzles us: what is a youthful-looking
Willie Donachie (second left) doing with them?

Well wrapped up against
the weather - and with
warming medicine in a
brown paper bag - here are
some optimistic Blues at
Piccadilly station setting
off for the 1970 League Cup
Final at Wembley. The gentleman in the suede coat
with fur collar (right) was
obviously ready to travel
on the same train I was on.
The heating didn't work
and it snowed all the way
to London.

Four years later and it's off to Wembley again for another League Cup final. City fan Harold Wrigley and his friends are engrossed in the *Manchester Evening News* Wembley souvenir edition, but would have less to smile about after the game as Wolves won 2-1.

The words 'dedication' and 'City fans' go hand in hand, and they didn't come any more dedicated than these three fans from Didsbury who travelled by car in 1978 to see the Blues play AC Milan in the famous San Siro stadium. The travelling fans, Derek Gould, Kenny Clements lookalike Anthony Saxton and Alan Fildes lived in the car for nine days and cooked on a primus stove.

And yet a third League Cup final, this time in 1976. Splendidly decked out in their City gear are the Highcock family from Haughton Green, Denton, clearly bubbling with confidence about the outcome. In the picture are Keith and Maureen Highcock, grandma Violet Bancroft, children Karen and Karl and Karen's boy-friend, Martin Capper.

Pictured on the Maine Road forecourt are the victorious members of the Abbey Hey branch of the Supporters' Club who have emerged winners of the club's quiz competition on all sports. Left to right are captain Kevin Davies, John Bullock, Kevin Dermody and Tom Evans. Abbey Hey beat Hadfield in the final, the competition attracting 12 branches.

In 1988, the Support Club took part in a seven-a-side tournament in Huddersfield and won a competition which had been dominated by Liverpool for the previous six years. The lads who won all six of their matches are (back row, left to right) Alan Corbishley (president), Thomas Williams (manager), John Barrow, Graham Woods, Dave Clarke and Keith Bailey (coach). At the front are Keith Brooks, Len Grimshaw, captain Gordon Woods and Derek Holland.

It's amazing the things City fans come up with to brighten the occasion. This momentous occasion was at Christmas time 1988 and, encouraged by a fanzine, Blues' supporters turned up in fancy dress for a game at the Victoria Ground, Stoke. Shown here complete with bananas are Rawtenstall-based Leonard Hilton, Yvonne Berry, Nicola Alderson, Chris Dalton and Phil Johnson.

'Who called me Hildegarde?' this unidentified fan appears to be asking as he looks in vain for the guy who wolf-whistled. The plaits wouldn't have been so obvious if he'd left the helmet off. Would they?

A chilly day in November 1988 as is obvious by the warm coats and bobble-hats. Here a group of City fans queue up for tickets for a forthcoming game with one turning away from the selling-point with a broad smile on his face and a ticket in his hand.

It's the last day of the Kippax and the City worshippers say farewell to their heroes at the end of the game. Some have even dug the bananas out of the attic for an airing

Ella Cummins, nine-year old daughter of ace *NME* photographer Kevin Cummins, seen here at one of City's soccer summer schools. Ella, always a keen City fan since her dad took her to Maine Road games, was one of only three girls in a sea of boys' faces, but soon found she was as good as most and better than some at the sport.

No, these three young City fans aren't auditioning for parts in *Macbeth* with 'Hubble, bubble, toil and trouble'. They're simply declaring their undying devotion to Manchester City through the popular art of face-painting, with the two young ladies in particular fixing their dreams on future successes.

Just about visible in this sea of excited youngsters are Junior Blues Chairman Ian Niven with chief scout Harry Godwin, taken at Christmas time 1981 at the annual Junior Blues pantomime in the Social Club. Can you put any names to the young faces?

'I've lost me dad', this worried-looking young man is telling Pc D48 back in 1972. Does anybody know who the boy is?

A memorable day out for seven-year old Matthew Coram from Marple and his brother Christopher, who were the Blues' mascots for this League game against Millwall in 1989. Matthew won the prize in a draw in *Manchester Evening News* Family stand and naturally wanted Christopher along with him on the big day. Steve Redmond and Clive Allen lead out the City team.

Manchester City's celebrity fans are practically all home grown, unlike those of some more 'trendy' clubs. Kevin Kennedy (Curly Watts in *Coronation Street*) and Bruce Jones (Les Battersby in the *Street*) are passionate City fans, seen here modelling new Kappa casual wear.

Manchester superstars Oasis are the latest in a long line of City fans who make their living in rock'n'roll. Others include Mike Pickering of M People, Johnny Marr (The Smiths), Mark E. Smith (The Fall), Billy Duffy of The Cult and Rick Wakeman of The Strawbs and Yes.

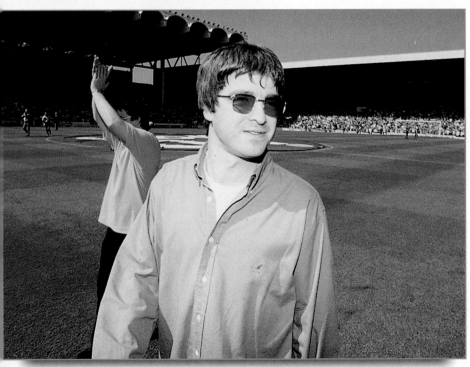

And blending rock'n'roll with radio is Marc 'Lard' Riley, formerly of The Fall and The Creepers, and now with fellow blue Mark Radcliffe on Radio 1, here wearing the new Kappa kit.

A number of City fans ply the airwaves with their passion, including James H. Reeve (see Foreword), GMR's Jimmy Wagg, pictured here with Tony Coton, and former Radio 1 DJ Andy Peebles.

It seems to be *de rigeur* for politicians to support good football (Mellor, Major, and Banks are the exception: they support Chelsea) and Greater Manchester MEP Glyn Ford is Maine Road's main man. Here he is pictured with Colin Barlow.

City provide a lot of dour black humour, which is probably why Manc comedians like Bernard Manning (captured here in pre-season training), Eddie Large and Chris Sievey (Frank Sidebottom) are such big fans.

141

Here is a classic from the archive, discovered in an obscure pile of old pictures. The two lads are in Bilbao, Northern Spain in 1969/70 for a European Cup-Winners clash, having hitch-hiked for six days. On the left is 16-year-old Rob Gretton, who later managed New Order and owned the Haçienda, arguably one of the world's most famous clubs. Whatever happened to Brian Andrews, aged 17? Another pop mogul to support City is Elliot Rashman, who took Mick Hucknall and Simply Red to superstardom.

The world of business is represented by Howard Davies, former head of the CBI (interestingly, his opposite number at the TUC, John Monks, is a Red), and recently Deputy Governor of the Bank of England. Then there's the City board, of course.

We know he's a Red, but actually he's a Blue! Centre-half David May has been a City supporter since being a kid. And Ryan Giggs was a Junior Blue. Arsenal full-back Lee Dixon is another Blue in red.

Blue becomes him… TV presenter John Stapleton, pictured here in a City blue jacket with his wife Lynn Faulds Wood, is a former *Blue Peter* stalwart.

Have you been paying attention? Here's the place to check your total recall of the contents of the book by testing yourself with the following 50 questions. Some of them are very easy indeed, others are quite tough (but the answers are in here somewhere) and a few - just a few - are not answered in the previous pages at all and require a bit of hard work.

This is because there is a fantastic prize to give away, and we have to whittle a few of you out. If you get over 45 answers you are pretty sure about, it's worth sending an entry in because we aren't expecting a perfect score.

The deadline is 1 May 1998, and the most correct entry received by then will win a pair of season tickets worth £250 each (yes, £500 worth of season ticket!) for the Platt Lane Stand. The winner will be announced in the June 1998 City Magazine, with their photo in the July issue.

To enter, write the answers on a piece of paper, pop them in an envelope and post them to: The Dead Good Dead Hard Manchester City Quiz, 164 Deansgate, Manchester M60 2RD. Normal City Magazine rules apply, mainly the one about the judges' decision being final, and the one about no cash equivalent. Note: Known record-keepers, statisticians etc... this quiz is not for you. We know who you are!

1. Who is City's most-capped player?

2. Which two City players starred with Pele in the film *Escape to Victory*?

3. Which City goalkeeper, playing at centre-forward with a broken finger, scored an equaliser against Bury in 1964?

4. When City beat Huddersfield Town 10-1 in 1987, who scored a single goal for City while three of his team-mates scored a hat-trick apiece?

5. In which season did Francis Lee score a record number of penalties for the club?

6. Who was the Blues' first million pound player?

7. Which local League club did City goal-keeping legend Bert Trautmann manage?

8. Uwe Rosler was top scorer in the 1996-97 season. How many League goals did he score?

9. In the last game of the 1996-97 season against Reading, which City defender scored an own goal?

10. City have had two famous cricketers in the first team. One of them scored a goal in the 1956 Cup Final. Who is he?

11. What was Kaziu Deyna's nationality?

12. In what year was the Central League (now the Pontin's League) launched?

13. To which club did Michel Vonk go on loan in the 1995-96 season?

14. Which member of the Royal Family visited Hyde Road to see City versus Liverpool in March 1920?

15. When Grimsby Town had fish and Bury had black puddings, what did City have?

16. Who was Joe Mercer's first signing in 1965?

17. Which City player suffered a serious injury in the 1955 Cup Final, one that ended his career?

Manchester City's Junior Blues organisation was born in 1974, and became the envy of all other clubs in the League, many of which went on to create their own similar outfits. Pictured here celebrating the JB's 20th anniversary are the then secretary, Mrs Jesse Ward, Francis Lee and Junior Blues chairman Ian Niven.

18. Who were the 'victims' when Trevor Francis scored two goals on his City debut?

19. From which club did full-back Andy Hill sign?

20. Name the Scottish player, signed by City in 1949, whose only games for the Blues were on the European mainland.

21. In 1995-96 season there were two ever-presents in City's League side. Who were they?

22. Name the Scottish club to whom City paid a record fee in 1973 for goalkeeper Keith Macrae?

23. How many times did City beat United in competitive games in 1954-55?

24. To which club was Terry Phelan transferred in 1995?

25. Which City player shared the Footballer of the Year award with Dave McKay in 1969?

26. Name the player who was capped by both Eire and Northern Ireland after World War Two.

27. From which Georgian club did Gio Kinkladze sign?

28. Can you name the season when City first erected floodlights at Maine Road?

29. Who were the two former City players who led Oldham Athletic into the Premiership?

30. In 1957-58 which City player scored 11 goals in 10 consecutive League games?

31. Who moved from City to Blackburn Rovers in March 1996?

32. Can you name the player who was signed from Sunderland in the 1970s along with Dennis Tueart?

33. How many times have City won the Lancashire Youth Cup?

34. Who was the first substitute used in a City League game in 1965?

35. Where in Germany was Uwe Rösler born?

The day that will remain etched into memories of all the City fans who were present. It's the famous 5-1 derby tory in 1989, and h is Trevor Morley to ing away City's se ond goal. Gary Pallister's express tells that he knows just where that ba going.

36. Who scored two goals on his City debut in the 1969 Charity Shield?

37. Who has made the highest number of League appearances for City...

38. ...and who has scored the highest number of League goals for the Blues?

39. Asa Hartford gained 36 Scottish caps with City. How many did he gain overall?

40. What was remarkable about the Goals column in the final League table of 1957-58 as far as City were concerned?

41. In which town were Chris Greenacre and Lee Crooks born?

42. Name the Norwegian who scored a hat-trick against Leicester City in the FA Cup in January 1994.

43. How many times have City Reserves won the Central League?

44. In which city was Colin Viljoen born?

45. How many London clubs did Clive Allen sign for during his career?

46. Which Manchester United manager had a son who signed for City?

47. For which German club did Michael Frontzeck sign in the 1996-97 season?

48. From which club did City sign star players Freddy Tilson and Eric Brook?

49. Name Scott Hiley's first League club.

50. In 1908-09 City had a young player on the books who made just 2 League appearances. He went on to play soccer for other clubs, but also played cricket for Middlesex and England, appearing in 83 Test innings for the latter. Who was he?